CONTENTS

Photo on the cover:
Klisoura Gorge, Cave 4. View of the entrance of the cave (*photo M. Kaczanowska*)

Eurasian Prehistory, 2 (2): 3–12.

PEBBLE SEMICIRCLE STRUCTURE FROM A LOWER PALEOLITHIC SITE IN SOUTHERN CHINA

Yingsan Fang[1], Yunping Huang[2] and Chen Shen[3]

[1] *Archaeology Institute of Nanjing Museum; 321 East Zhongshan Road, Nanjing City, Jiangsu Province, PRC, 210016, ysfang@xinhuanet.com*
[2] *Department of Archaeology, Peking University; Beijing, PRC, 100871, yunping@163bj.com*
[3]*Department of World Cultures, Royal Ontario Museum; 100 Queen's Park, Toronto, ON, Canada, M5S 2C6, chens@rom.on.ca*

Abstract

An area of hominid activity, a pebble semicircle structure, was identified in the Maozhushan site in Ningguo, Anhui Province, prompting a study of lower Paleolithic human behavior in southern China. The semicircle structure was recovered with a series of small pebble circles within and with stone tool artifacts. The site formation study points to minimal natural modification at the site, suggesting some degree of human intention in the organization of the structure. Geostratigraphic and comparative ESR dates suggest that the age of the site falls between the Late Lower Pleistocene and the early Middle Pleistocene. Given the evidence at present, the Maozhushan site may have been a central campsite of the Shuiyangjiang River Paleolithic complex recently identified in Lower Yangtze River of China.

INTRODUCTION

Hominid behaviors of the Lower Paleolithic have been the subject of many studies by archaeologists and paleoanthropologists. Cultural remains appearing on sites in a patterned distribution in a relatively primary context and in association with lithic technology are usually inferred to reflect hominid living adaptation strategies (see papers in Petraglia and Korisettar, 1998). However, scientists have identified very few structural remains in Lower Paleolithic sites that show purposeful construction and which would suggest a cognitive development and behavior pattern of early hominids. Nevertheless, some archaeological evidence indicates that structures were built by hominids in the Lower and Middle Pleistocene periods.

For example, in Bilzingsleben, Germany, Middle Pleistocene localities with patterned distributions of artifacts and faunal remains were found. Two circular concentrations of lithic artifacts were identified concurrently with large stones and bones, providing possible evidence of a structure foundation (Mania, 1986, 1991). Another of this kind, the Terra Amata site in Nice, France, was initially thought to be an Acheulian Shelter, although later research suggested that site modification was likely the result of natural agency (Lumley, 1969; Villa, 1983). Similar patterned arrangements or concentrations of stones and bones were also identified at sites like Latamne in Syria (Clarke, 1967, 1968) and Olorgesailie in Kenya (Isaac, 1977), but the formation of artifacts could be attributed to natural processes, rather than intentional hominid behavior.

Recently, similar features suggesting Paleolithic settlements have been found in southern China. The excavations of the Jigongshan site in Hubei Province unearthed a 500 m^2 living floor, revealing an accumulation of thousands of stone artifacts and pebbles in circular patterns. The excavators propose that it might have been a

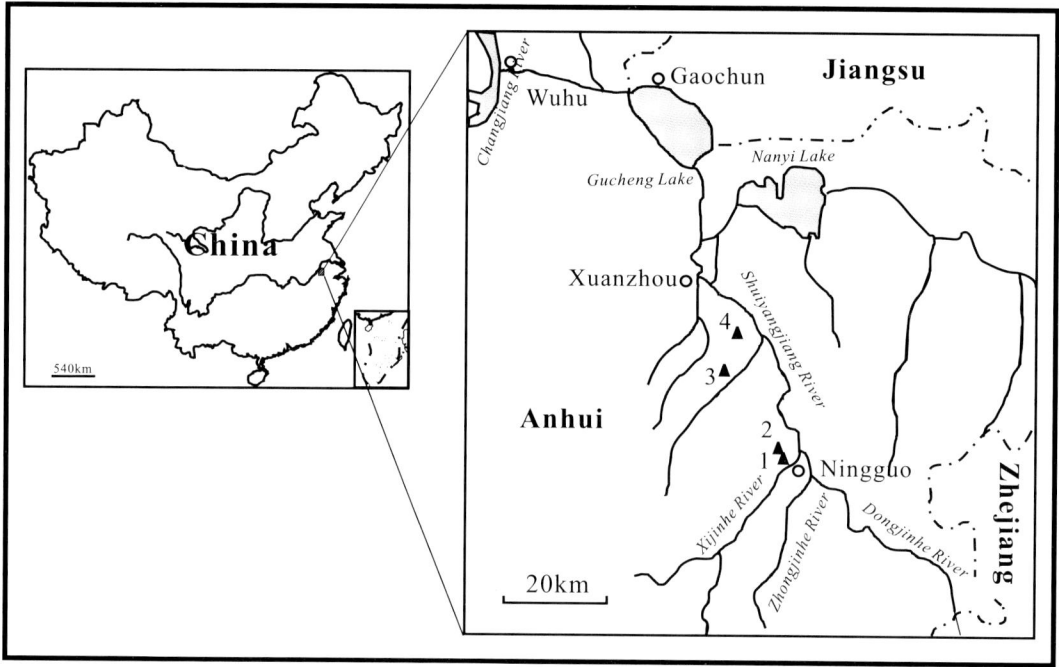

Fig. 1. Map of China, showing locations of sites discussed in the text: 1) Maozhushan; 2) Guanshan; 3) Wuli-peng; 4) Chenshan

seasonal campsite or workshop during the early Upper Pleistocene (Wang, 1999, 2003; Liu and Wang, 2001). In this report, we will introduce another discovery from southern China – a pebble semicircular occupation of the Lower Paleolithic.

MAOZHUSHAN SITE AND STRATIGRAPHY

The Maozhushan (Bamboo Hill) site was first identified in 1996 and excavated the following year. Beneath a 3 m thick layer of net-patterned red clay, a typical geoformation of the Middle Pleistocene in southern China, the excavators found a cultural deposit. Due to the stunning discovery of a large pebble semicircle, the entire site was re-surveyed and lithic artifacts were analyzed in 1998. The results of this preliminary investigation are described below.

This site is located 4.5 km northwest of Ningguo City, Anhui Province (Fig. 1), on riverine terrain about 65 m above sea level. The settlement lies on the second terrace (T2) of the Shuiyangji-ang River, a second tributary of the Lower Yangtze River, where three upstream rivers (Xijihe River, Zhongjinhe River, and Dongjinhe River) join to form the Shuiyangjiang River. The site covers hilly landscape of nearly 4,000 m², of which an area of 13-x-15 m² was exposed in 1997 winter field season.

The sediments were divided into four layers (Fig. 2). From top to bottom: 1) yellow silt clay layer 1.5 m thick; 2) a brownish red silt clay layer with grayish white lacework, commonly called the net-patterned red clay 3.3 m thick. Cultural remains were identified at the bottom of this layer; 3) grayish white sandy clay with numerous weathered pebbles, less than 1 m thick. The sediment contained a large quantity of grayish white lacework gradually getting thinner from the north to the south; and 4) quartz sandstone of Devonian bedrock about 10 m thick. Our analysis suggested that the top two layers (layers 1–2) were probably eolian dust deposits. Layer 3 might be an alluvial flooding deposit. Layer 4 was fluviolacustrine sediment (Yang *et al.*, 1991).

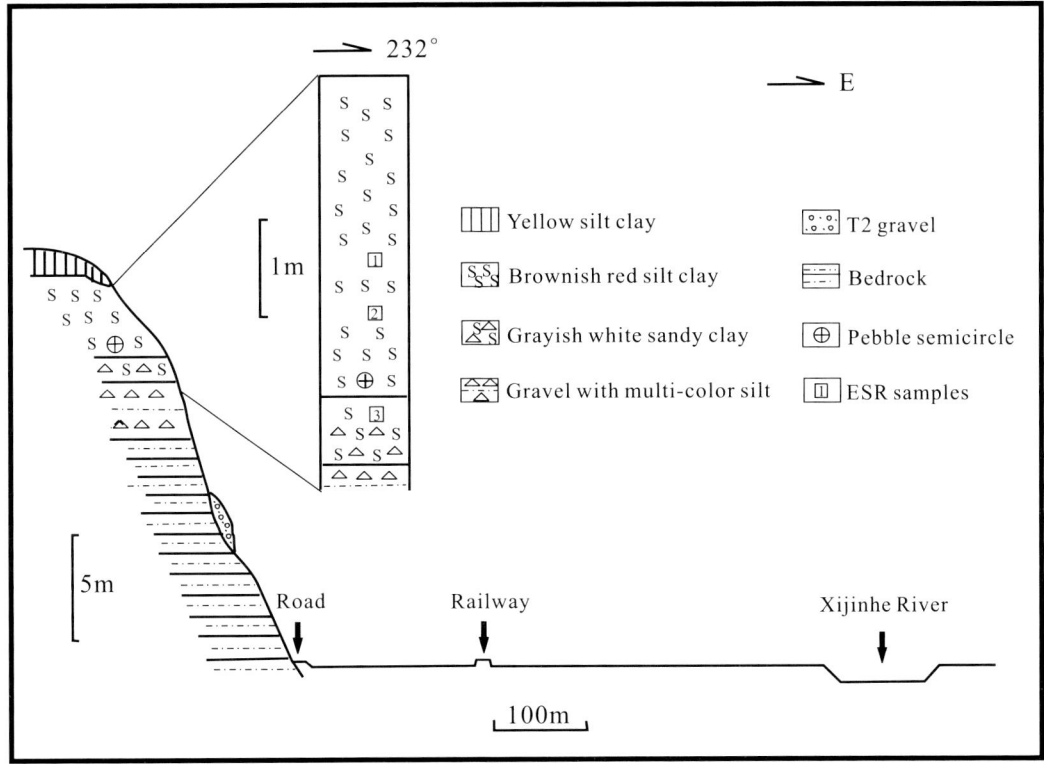

Fig. 2. Stratigraphic section of Maozhushan sediment

PEBBLE SEMICIRCLE

The most notable discovery is a large stone structure made of more than 1,100 pebbles (Fig. 3). This feature has a semicircular shape with a 10 m long east–west axis; the short axis is 6 m long. Over 100 stone artifacts were recovered; however no faunal remains were found.

The opening of the pebble semicircle faces northeast. The western edge of the structure measures about 7.4 m long from the northern point to the extreme southern point and the eastern edge is about 3.3 m long. Inside the structure is an open space about 4.7-x-4 m^2, where no pebbles or artifacts were found. At least 1,167 individual pebbles were counted constituting the stone edge ring that is as wide as 2 m. The height of the stone ring varies, inclining from southwest to northeast along the long axis. It is assumed that the opening of semicircle was intended to face the river valley.

The stone ring was made primarily with a single layer of stones; only a few double layers of pebbles were found in some segments. One segment that was constructed with three layers of pebbles was identified in the excavation square C4.

The pebbles were principally composed of quartz sandstone and feldspar sandstone (85.5%). Others included quartzite (7.8%), siliceous (4.6%), and flint, vein quartz, and limestone (0.6%). The average pebble size was 81 mm long, 60 mm wide, and 39 mm thick. The percentages of sub-roundness, roundness, and super-roundness of the pebbles accounted for 44.1%, 36.4%, and 6.7%, respectively. Most pebbles showed no weathering (64.9%), while slightly weathered and heavily weathered pebbles accounted for 29.3% and 5.8%, respectively. These percentages implied that for the structure, the hominids at the Maozhushan site might have selected pebbles for raw materials that had a rounded, large size, and no weathered or slightly weathered pebbles.

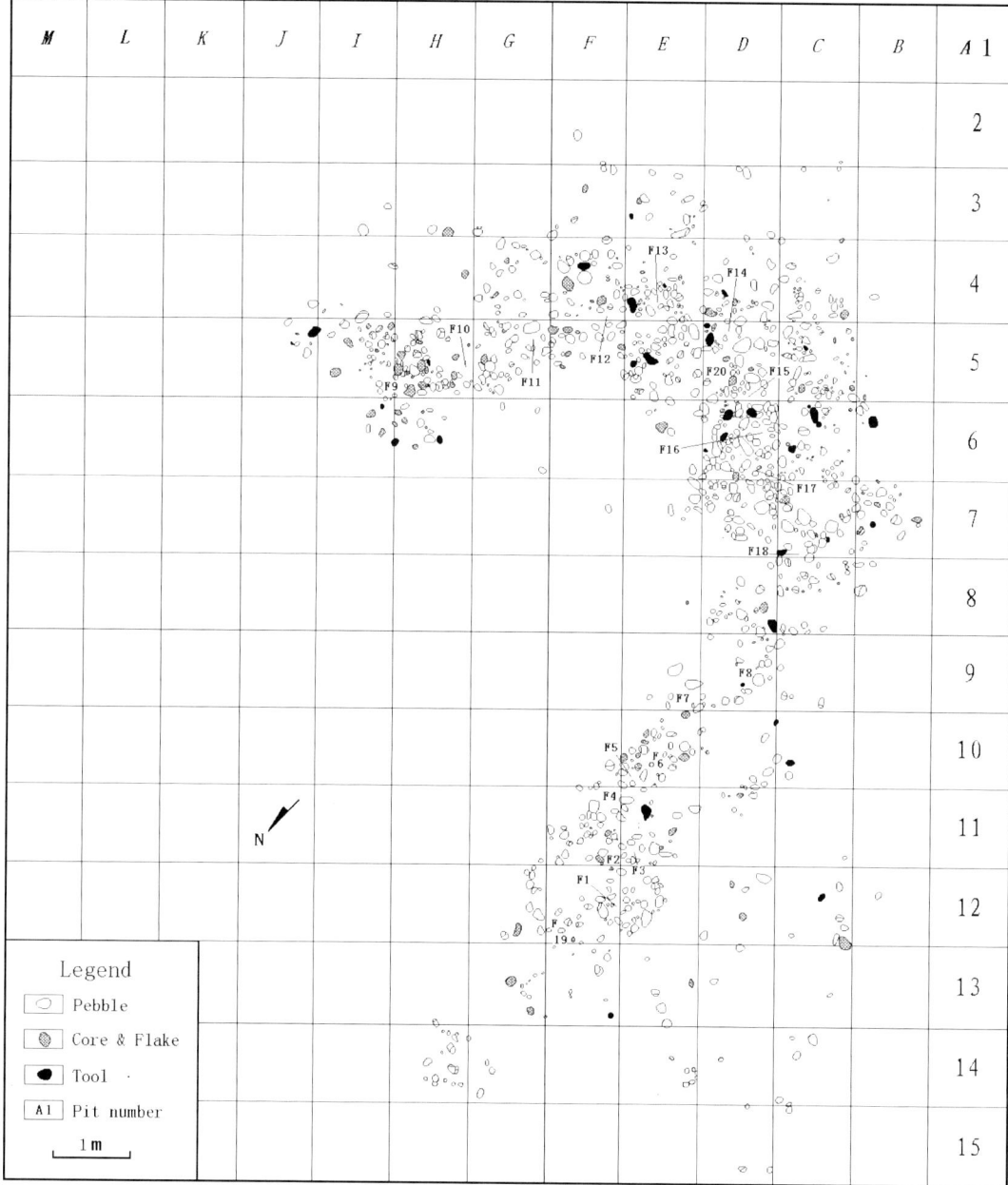

Fig. 3.   Plan view of pebble semicircle at the Maozhushan site

SMALL PEBBLE CIRCLES

What is more interesting about this discovery is that twenty small pebble circles, ranging 20–30 cm in diameter, were found on the edge of the pebble semicircle. The outer edges of these small pebble circles were parts of the pebble ring structure, leasving a small hollow center. Most of the inner circles were regular in shape, and others irregular. Lithic artifacts were recovered from nine of the small circles (Fig. 4).

In the samples taken from two small circles

Fig. 4. Examples of small pebble circles at the Maozhushan site

(F9 and F20), we noticed that sediments within the features were the same texture and color as the sediments outside the small circles. No charcoal or faunal remains were found inside. These circles might have been the remains of post moulds but no direct evidence permitted us to point to this hypothesis. The samples of sediment taken from inside the circles were analyzed at the Structure Center of the University of Science and Technology of China, and the result suggested that the chemical composition of carbon, hydrogen, and nitrogen within the sediment had no great different from those outside circles. The function of these small pebble circles needs to be further investigated.

STONE ARTIFACTS

A total of 154 stone artifacts were recovered from the pebble semicircle at the Maozhushan

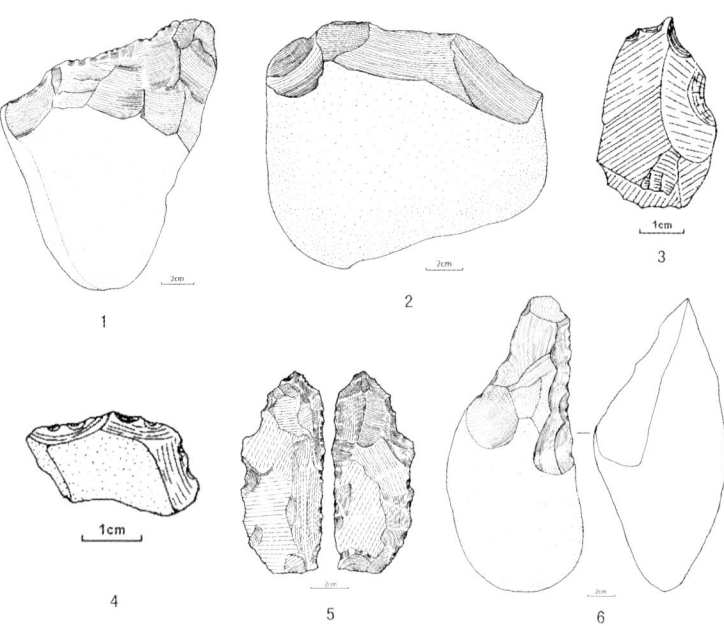

Fig. 5.   Lithic artifacts from the Maozhushan site: 1) pick; 2) chopper; 3) drill; 4) scraper; 5) point; 6) pick

site. They were scattered evenly throughout the structure and no patterned clusters of lithic artifacts could be identified. Typologically, the lithic assemblage primarily consisted of chunks (31.9%), cores (24.7%), and flakes (19.5%). Tool types included scrapers, hammers, choppers, points, picks, spheroids, and drills (Figs. 5–6). Most of these tools were made on pebble cores, with only eleven pieces made on flakes (eight scrapers and three points). The sizes of the stone tools thus are relatively large, with average length, width, thickness at 82 mm, 69 mm, and 43 mm, respectively (Table 1).

The stone artifacts show generally similar characteristics with the pebbles of the semicircle in size, raw materials, and weathering condition. The raw materials for making these stone tools were primarily quartz sandstone and feldspar sandstone, followed by quartzite, quartz, chert, and the others. While the percentage of stone tools made of quartz sandstone and quartzite (70.1% and 13.6%) was higher than that of pebbles from the semicircle structure, feldspar sandstone was lower (5.2%). The degree of weathering displayed by the raw materials showed no great difference from that of the semicircle pebbles. This similarity may indicate that the raw materials

for both lithic artifacts and semicircle pebbles might have been obtained from the same place, and that the pebbles might have been intentionally selected as raw material for tool production.

SITE FORMATION IN RELATION TO THE NATURE OF PEBBLE SEMICIRCLE

A portion of the pebble semicircle overlapped directly the gravel of layer 4, and thus we question whether the formation of this feature was the result of nature causes. We compared both the lithic artifacts and the semicircle pebbles to pebbles from two other sources: one source was the underlying gravel from Layer 4; and the other source was Terrace 2 (T2) gravel sediment of the Shuiyangjiang River near the southeastern hill slope of Maozhushan. The raw material types, degree of weathering, and degree of roundness suggest some difference and similarities.

Fifty-one samples randomly selected from the underlying gravel layer show that the average size of raw materials fall between that of the semicircle and T2 gravel pebbles. The raw material types were similar to the semicircle pebbles. It is also suggested that the degree of weathering was

Fig. 6. Lithic artifacts from the Maozhushan site: 1) chopper; 2) pick; 3) point; 4) chopper; 5) point; 6) drill; 7) scraper; 8) pick; 9) point. Scale bar = 1 cm

heavier than that of the semicircle pebbles, but that the roundness was weaker. Secondly, samples of 45 pebbles from T2 gravel suggested that their average sizes were the smallest among the three compared groups. The difference was that

82.2% of pebbles from this group were quartz sandstone, and 17.8% are siliceous. The materials of this group displayed the heaviest roundness and light weathering.

In general, the average sizes of the semicir-

Table 1

Lithic artifacts from the Maozhushan site

Class	N	%	Mean length mm	Mean width mm	Mean thickness
Core	38	24.7	85	93	85
Flake	30	19.5	57	50	18
Chunk	49	31.9	80	55	26
Hammer	6	3.9	101	66	30
Chopper	10	6.5	138	120	51
Scraper	8	5.2	49	51	20
Point	3	1.9	60	36	18
Pick	5	3.2	170	110	72
Spheroids	4	2.6	77	67	57
Drill	1	0.6	40	30	18
Total	**154**	100	82	69	43

cle's pebbles were the largest. The measurements were closer to those of the pebbles from the underlying gravel than they were from the T2 gravel. The physical features of the raw material of the semicircle pebbles were also more similar to that of the underlying gravel than they were to the T2 gravel. However, the difference was the lower degree of weathering found in the semicircle pebbles than the underlying gravel, and the roundness was higher. It was suggested that the materials of the pebble semicircle might have been obtained from the underlying gravel.

The geomorphological study of the Shuiyangjiang River suggested that the net-patterned red clay was the result of a continuous process of eolian-dust accumulation (Fang *et al.*, 1992; Li *et al.*, 1997). Therefore the pebble semicircle from layer 2 could not have been formed by river alluvium or other natural dynamics.

In addition, the pebble semicircle was formed in regular geometric shapes with hollow centers and zigzag contour edges. The spaces between each pebble of the structure were filled with pure clay without granule gravel. Most portions of the edges were lined up with single layer of pebbles. The evidence suggested an intentional arrangement by a hominid.

During the 1997–1998 field seasons, we also surveyed the site by digging 22 1 m² test pits along with one 7-x-5 m excavation unit. Each test pit was 10–15 m apart. No more pebble structures or other features were found; neither were there found similar pebble clusters that were formed by natural causes. For this reason, we believe that hominids might have built the pebble semicircle for special purposes, but its function remains unknown at present.

DATE OF THE PEBBLE SEMICIRCLE

It is unfortunate that there were no faunal remains found in the pebble semicircle, which could have been sampled directly for ERS dating. However, we selected two samples from the middle section and bottom section of the net-patterned red clay layer, respectively, which encompassed the deposit of the structure, and one additional sample from the underlying layer (Fig. 2). The ESR dating results by the Structure Centre of University of Science and Technology of China suggested age ranges from about 420 Kyr, 631 Kyr and 665 Kyr, respectively (Table 2). Thus, the age of the pebble semicircular structure was estimated to be around 631 ka BP.

Furthermore, the Chenshan site, about 27 km northwest of Maozhushan, yielded a number of ESR dates. One sample taken from the middle–lower section of the same type of sediment as the red clay layer of Maozhushan had an age of 680 ka BP (Fang, 1997). Ten samples obtained

Table 2

ESR dating from the Maozhushan site

Original number	Laboratory number	Layer	Depth cm	Age Kyr
1	NGD1A	middle section of Layer 2	200	420
2	30NGD2A	bottom section of Layer 2	250	631.2
3	NGD3A	upper section of Layer 4	330	664.9

from the top to the bottom of the sediment provided dates ranging between 126 and 817 ka BP (Yang *et al.*, 1996). In addition, a few paleomagnetic dates from the gravel layer in the Lushan Mountain area (equivalent to the underlying gravel at the Maozhushan site) suggested the deposit beneath the structure is no older than 900 ka BP (Xing, 1989). Lithio-stratigraphy in the study region indicated that layer 1 of the Maozhushan site is equivalent to the upper part of the Chenshan deposit, belonging to the late Middle Pleistocene. The Maozhushan layer 2, equivalent to the lower part of the Chenshan deposits, should fall between the late Lower Pleistocene and the early Middle Pleistocene.

SUMMARY

Thus far, the more than 20 Paleolithic localities recently identified in the Shuiyangjiang River Valley comprise the first Paleolithic settlement concentration in the lower reaches of the Yangtze River (Fang *et al.*, 1992). These sites were found within a 1,500 km² area that included Chenshan, Guanshan, and Wulipeng (Fig. 1) – possible large open campsites. The discovery of the Maozhushan site in 1996 revealed an important open campsite of the Middle Pleistocene in the study region. The Lower Paleolithic structure at Maozhushan is the earliest structure created by an early hominid ever found in China.

We cannot clearly interpret the function of this structure based on the current evidence. However, it should be noted that most of the pebbles are suitable for tool making. All pebbles for the semicircle structure were collected and transported by early hominids. Cores, flakes, hammers, and chunks accounted for 80.6% of all stone artifacts, indicative of possible on-site tool manufacture.

Some small circles together with stone artifacts present in the ring of the pebble semicircle could be evidence of the use of post moulds and a possible implication of the earliest wooden shelter. However, there is lack of faunal remains and the organic component of the sediment is no different from those outside the circles. One possibility could be that, due to acid earth in the study region of southern China, organic materials decomposed completely. It is evident that most feldspar sandstone pebbles *in situ* have been weathered badly.

Some tools showed traces of possible use. Macro-edge damaged stone tools (*n* = 21), a possible sign of use, accounted for 13.6% of the entire lithic assemblage. Specimen 1005 from Pit J5 had a pointed edge, placed upright and inserted into the clay with the point downward when it was unearthed. Based on this evidence we suggest that the pebble semicircle might have been a seasonal living structure where tool making activities were conducted; however the specific function of this structure needs further investigation. Judging from the evidence, the Maozhushan site may have been a central campsite of the Shuiyangjiang River Paleolithic complex.

Acknowledgements

We thank Professors Zhang Senshui, Wang Youping, Yang Dayuan, Wang Fubao, and Liang Renyou who provided us with very helpful assistance and suggestions during their visit at the site and the laboratory analysis. Our thanks to Dr. Chen Chun for his constructive comments and to Dr. Richard Cosgrove for his comments and editorial assistance.

REFERENCES

CLARKE J. D. 1967. The Middle Acheulian occupation site at Latamne, northern Syria, I. *Quaternaria*, 9, 1–69.

CLARKE J. D. 1968. The Middle Acheulian occupation site at Latamne, northern Syria, II. Further excavation (1965): General results, definition, and interpretation. *Quaternaria*, 10, 1–71.

FANG Y. 1997. A report of excavation at Chenshan locality in 1988 in Anhui Province. *Acta Anthropologica Sinica*, 16, 96–106.

FANG Y., YANG D., HAN H., ZHOU L. 1992. Taphonomic study of Paleolithic locality group of Shuiyangjiang River. *Acta Anthropologica Sinica*, 11, 134–142.

Isaac G. L. 1977. *Olorgesailie*. University of Chicago Press, Chicago.

LI X., YANG D., LU H., HAN H. 1997. The grain-size features of Quaternary an eolian-dust deposition sequence in southern Anhui and their significance. *Marine Geology & Quaternary Geology*, 17, 73–82.

LIU D., WANG Y. 2001. A preliminary report on the excavation of Jigongshan site. *Acta Anthropologica Sinica*, 20, 102–114.

LUMLEY H. de 1969. A Paleolithic camp at Nice. *Science American*, 220, 42–50.

MANIA D. 1986. Die Forschungsgrabung bei Bilzingsleben. *Jahresschrift für Mitteldeutsche Vorgeschichte*, 69, 235–255.

MANIA D. 1991. Les premiers peuplements humains dans la région de Saale-Elbe. In: E. Bonifay, B. Vandermeersch (ed.) *Les premiers Européens*. Éditions du Comité des Travaux Historiques et Scientifiques, Paris, 173–175.

PETRAGLIA M. D., KORISETTAR R. 1998. *Early human behavior in Global Context: the rise and diversity of the Lower Palaeolithic record*. Routledge, London and New York.

VILLA P. 1983. *Terra Amata and the Middle Pleistocene archaeological record of southern France*. University of California Press, Berkeley and Los Angeles.

WANG Y. 1999. The Jigongshan site. In: *The important discoveries of Archaeology in China in 1998*, Cultural Relics Publishing House, Beijing, 38–40.

WANG Y. 2003. New Palaeolithic discoveries in the Middle Yangzi River region, China. In: C. Shen, S. Keates (ed) *Current Research in Chinese Pleistocene Archaeology*. BAR International Series S1179, Archaeopress:Oxford, 57–66.

XING, L. 1989. Magnetostratigraphic age of Quaternary glaciations in the Lushan area. *Bulletin of the Institute of Geomechanics*, 13, 71–77.

YANG D., HANG H., ZHOU L., FANG Y. 1991. Eolian deposit and environmental change of middle-late Pleistocene in Xuancheng, Anhui Province South of the lower reaches of the Yangtze River. *Marine Geology & Quaternary Geology*, 11, 97–104.

YANG H., ZHAO O., LI X., XIA Y. 1996. ESR dating of eolian sediment and red earth series from Xuancheng profile in Anhui Province. *Acta Pedologica Sinica*, 33, 293–300.

Eurasian Prehistory, 2 (2): 13–31.

MAPPING GRAVETTIAN EASTERN EUROPE: CEJKOV AND EASTERN SLOVAK SETTLEMENT IN CONTEXT

Silvia Tomášková[1], Ľubomíra Kaminská[2], Maria Hajnalová[3] and Dale Hudler[4]

[1] *University of North Carolina at Chapel Hill, USA; tomas@unc.edu;*
[2] *Archaeologický Ústav SAV Košice, Slovakia;*
[3] *Archaeologický Ústav SAV Nitra, Slovakia;*
[4] *University of Texas at Austin, USA*

Abstract

We present the results of a field project at Cejkov in eastern Slovakia, describing the location, geochronology and paleoenvironment of the site, and provide an overview of recovered materials. We also situate the site in the context of contemporaneous late Gravettian sites in central and eastern Europe. In presenting well-documented and dated sites from the region that fall within the range of 25–22 Kyr B.P., we wish to open a discussion of social interactions within and between regions. This essay aims to narrow the time frame in which Late Upper Paleolithic settlements in Europe are discussed, and put forth a database that allows the mapping of late Gravettian settlements.

INTRODUCTION

In this essay we wish to accomplish two tasks. First, we present the results of a field project at Cejkov in eastern Slovakia, describe the location, geochronology, and paleoenvironment, and present the recovered materials from the site. Second, we situate the site in the context of contemporaneous late Gravettian sites in central and eastern Europe. We present well-documented and dated sites from the region that fall within the range of 25–22 Kyr B.P. to open a discussion of social interactions within and between regions. This essay aims to narrow the time frame in which Late Upper Paleolithic settlements in Europe are discussed, and put forth a database that allows the mapping of late Gravettian settlements.

Paleolithic population settlements and movements in Europe just prior to and during the Last Glacial Maximum (LGM) have been the focus of renewed attention in recent years, and our knowledge has been greatly enhanced with new radiocarbon dates (e.g. Roebroeks *et al.*, 2000; Soffer and Gamble, 1990; Vasil'ev *et al.*, 2000). More precise dating, and the increase in the sheer number of known dates, has improved our understanding of the movements of prehistoric populations through the continent, as well as their adaptation to changing environments, their establishment of settlements in specific regions, and their abandonment of those sites with the deterioration of the climate during the LGM. However, most of our knowledge of the Upper Paleolithic has been based on data from well dated and documented sites in western Europe (and particularly southwestern Europe), then extended to apply to the continent as a whole. The Gravettian is the only exception where central Europe plays an important role. Sampling bias thus remains the major obstacle to regional studies and models of population dynamics between western, central, and eastern Europe, and in building hypotheses of migrations and interactions between groups within regions and across the continent.

The central European Upper Paleolithic has been mainly represented in the literature by the Moravian sites such as Dolní Vestonice, Pavlov,

Predmostí and Stránská skála (Svoboda, 1991; Svoboda *et al.*, 1996; Trinkaus *et al.*, 2000), to some degree by Austrian sites, such as Alberndorf (Bachner *et al.*, 1996; Trnka, 2004), Grubgraben (Montet-White, 1988, 1994), or Willendorf (Haesarts *et al.*, 1990, 1996), recently several German sites (e.g. Conard and Adler, 1997; Street and Terberger, 2000) and a few Hungarian sites (Dobosi, 2000a; Svoboda and Simán, 1989). The specific details and dates of the east European Upper Paleolithic, particularly from the former Soviet Union, have become much better known in the last decade (e.g., Allsworth-Jones, 1994; Anikovich, 1992; Borziac, 1997; Hoffecker, 1999, 2002; Iakovleva, 2000; Leonova, 1994; Vasilev *et al.*, 2000). Yet the connections, relationships, and routes between and within eastern, central, and western Europe remain sketchy, and largely based on assumptions. Considerable further research will be required for us to have a clearer picture of population movements and settlements just prior to the Last Glacial Maximum.

The generally accepted model suggests depopulation of most of Europe during the LGM (20–15 Kyr). However, attention has also been called to a need for investigation of microclimates, particularly in central Europe, preceding and during the LGM, which would have allowed either survival or occasional episodes of small scale occupation (Barton *et al.*, 2003; Street and Tarberger, 2000). This need to consider individual ecological niches encourages a more detailed look at particular micro-regions and their relationship with adjacent settings. Slovakia is one such region, which has received little attention in debates of prehistoric movements between eastern and western Europe or even within Europe in general. The west Slovak Váh river valley sites Moravany and Nitra-Čermáň are better known partly due to their proximity to the Moravian sites (Svoboda, 1991, 2000), and partly due to more recent renewed excavations (Hromada and Kozlowski, 1995; Kozlowski, 1998; Verpoorte, 2004). Eastern Slovakia on the other hand, while the focus of considerable Slovak archaeological research for the last four decades, is far less well known internationally, as the results of this work have either not been translated (e.g., Bánesz, 1989, 1990, 1996; Bárta, 1965) or the publications have been short survey reports without wide distribution. To provide a more detailed archaeological picture of central and eastern Europe, the authors engaged in an international collaborative project in eastern Slovakia in 2000 and 2001. The major contribution of this project is an establishment of a well-dated record for eastern Slovakia, providing a reference in discussions of migrations and population movements close to the last glacial maximum within this region and in eastern Europe in general.

GEOGRAPHY AND LOCATION

Eastern Slovakia lies at the intersection of several broad geographic regions of Europe: a north central region encompassing Germany, Poland and the Czech Republic; a northeastern region encompassing the Ukraine; and the Russian steppe zone, and southeastern region composed of Hungary, parts of Romania, and the Balkans. The Carpathian Mountains in the north and east of the region provide a physical barrier to the northern European Plain, the Baltic and the Russian steppe, while the Hungarian Plain to the south opens to the valleys of the Tisza and Danube rivers. The valleys of the Ondava and Topľa rivers constitute the main potential communication route between the Tisza basin and Carpathian passes leading to the Vistula basin. At the same time, the Uh and Latorica rivers that flow from east to west provide potential communication routes for the eastern Slovak lowland with the Ukraine, and with the mountain passes of the eastern Carpathians leading to the Dnester basin. This communication junction encouraged us to take particular interest in the territory of eastern Slovakia that includes the Topľa and Ondava basins (Fig. 1).

Cejkov is located in the catchment of the Ondava River, on the eastern slope of the Zemplín Mountains and in the southern part of the east Slovak Lowlands. It has received initial attention as a potential site of extensive Gravettian and Epigravettian occupations (Bánesz, 1976, 1980), and fit our general interest in settlement and interaction context of the region during the late Upper Paleolithic. The site of Cejkov is to the north of the village of the same name, on the slopes of the Tokaj hill, which is 158 m above sea level, an eastern outpost of the Zemplín range formed by rhyodacite minerals. It is bordered on the north

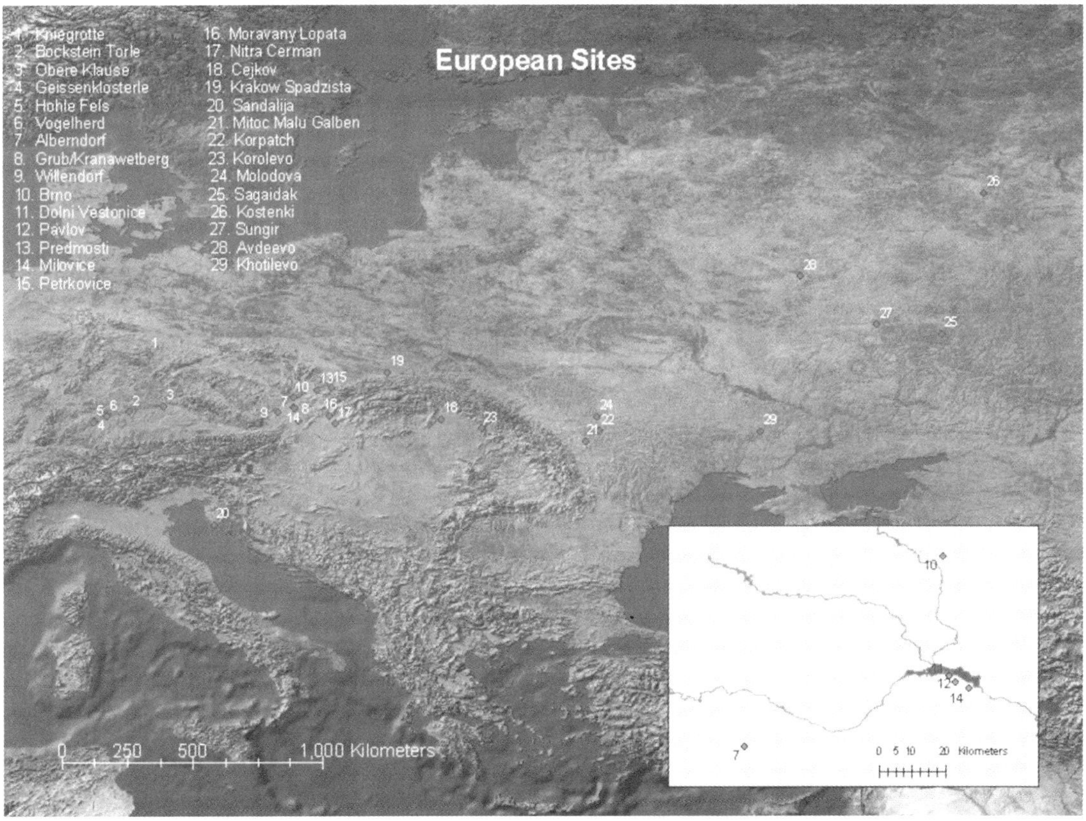
European Sites
1. Kniegrotte
2. Bockstein Torle
3. Obere Klause
4. Geissenklosterle
5. Hohle Fels
6. Vogelherd
7. Alberndorf
8. Grub/Kranawetberg
9. Willendorf
10. Brno
11. Dolni Vestonice
12. Pavlov
13. Predmosti
14. Milovice
15. Petrkovice
16. Moravany Lopata
17. Nitra Cerman
18. Cejkov
19. Krakow Spadzista
20. Sandalija
21. Mitoc Malu Galben
22. Korpatch
23. Korolevo
24. Molodova
25. Sagaidak
26. Kostenki
27. Sungir
28. Avdeevo
29. Khotilevo
0 250 500 1,000 Kilometers
0 5 10 20 Kilometers

Fig. 1. Distribution of central and east European Late Gravettian sites (22–25 Kyr)

side by the Lagaš tributary of the Ondava river, rising steeply about 30 m over the stream. Equally steep are the eastern and western slopes; only the southern slope has a moderate incline (Fig. 2).

LITHIC SOURCES

We began the project with a surface survey of the Ondava river valley further to the north, near the locality of Nižný Hrabovec (SE Slovakia, 48°51'N, 21°24'E) where surface collections of Paleolithic artifacts had been reported by local amateur archaeologists (Bánesz and Zubko, 1992). Four test trenches were made in order to determine the stratigraphic position and geomorphology of the finds, and observations were carried out in the neighboring natural profiles and industrial quarries. Materials from our surface collection and test pits were analyzed in terms of sourcing (Pawlikowski, 2000). The identified raw materials were classified in the following manner shown in Table 1.

The raw materials indicate a role of this area as a communication junction for Paleolithic occupants of central and eastern Europe. The long list of mesolocal and foreign raw materials allows us to suggest a broad range of interregional links in eastern Slovakia. Typologically the artifacts at

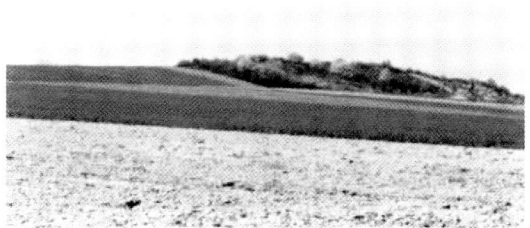

Fig. 2. Cejkov 2001, view of location on Tokaj Hill, eastern Slovakia

Table 1
Eastern Slovakia: Ondava river valley raw material classification

Classification	Distance (km)	Raw material	Source
Local	25-30	hornstone	Ondava river valley
Mesolocal	50-150	radiolarite, black menilithic hornostone	NE Slovakia
Mesolocal		radiolarite, obsidian, jasper	SE Slovakia, Hungarian border, Bükk mountains, Dnestr basin
Foreign	180-300	flint	middle Vistula river, upper Oder basin, Krakow-Czestochowa Jurassic Plateau
Foreign		chocolate flint	Holy Cross mountains
Foreign		andesite	Korolevo, Ukraine

Nižný Hrabovec displayed typological features ranging from Mousterian types, using the Quina and bifacial retouch, Levallois technology, Bohunician types that could potentially represent transitional industries, Aurignacian and Epi-aurignacian tool types, as well as a few Gravettian and Epi-gravettian diagnostic finds. The archaeological materials suggest a continuous presence of human groups in the area during the Middle and Upper Paleolithic. The stone tools also indicate that we are dealing with material remains of groups that were most likely highly mobile, and traveled to the north (present-day Poland), south (Hungary), and the east (the Ukraine), or had extensive social networks that allowed an exchange of information and/or materials (Bárta, 1965; Kaminská, 1991). Previous geoarchaeological investigations of the region revealed its importance as a source of radiolarite, and particularly obsidian that was transported to sites in central and eastern Europe during the Paleolithic, and even more extensively in later Neolithic times (Harčár *et al.*, 1995/96; Kaminská, 1991; Williams and Nandris, 1977; Williams-Thorpe, *et al.* 1984).

While our initial surface collections at Nižný Hrabovec suggested a rich potential for the Ondava river valley, the subsequent test pits also indicated a significant postdepositional disturbance, solifluction, and soil movement that precluded any possibility of a clear stratigraphic picture. Consequently we relocated during the following season further south along the Ondava River to Cejkov (48°28'N, 21°46'E), a locality that has been originally excavated by Bánesz, in a close proximity to another known Paleolithic locality – Kašov. The field project at Cejkov confirmed that the analysis of the raw material sources from Nižný Hrabovec can be applied to the region of eastern Slovakia as a whole, confirming the status of the region as an intersection between east and west and north and south.

CEJKOV: GEOCHRONOLOGY AND PALEOENVIRONMENTAL SETTING

The research at Cejkov was informed by previous work in the area by Bánesz, carried out intermittently since the 1960s until the late 1980s (Bánesz, 1969, 1976, 1980, 1990, 1996; Bánesz and Pieta, 1961). The five excavation units that we carried out were placed in relation to earlier units by Bánesz, relying on his records and maps. Soil analysis of samples from the units indicated that soil movements, postdepositional changes and solifluction seriously affected the area and only excavation unit 1 had stratigraphy that was reliable and well preserved. This unit contained a number of lithic artifacts, bone fragments and two features; archeobotanical and soil samples were taken from here for a detailed paleoenvironmental reconstruction (Hajnalová) and soil analysis (Fig. 3).

The soil analysis of the cultural level in excavation unit 1, deposited in a calcareous loess, suggests that the Gravettian occupation at Cejkov occurred before the Tursac interstadial. The layer produced abundant (in numbers as well as in volume) charcoal fragments of coniferous trees or

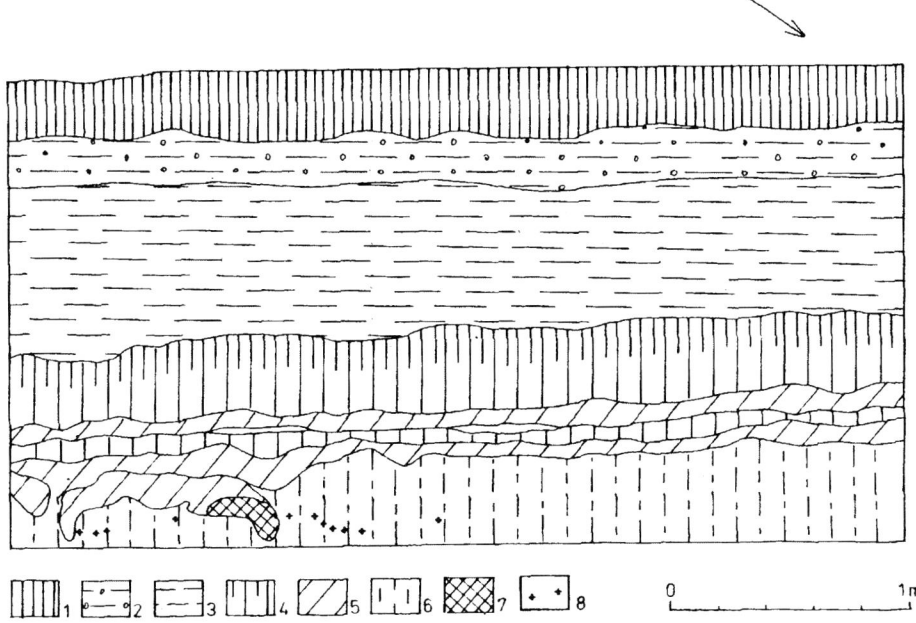

Fig. 3. Cejkov, excavation unit 1/2001, western profile

shrubs, and spruce (*Picea abies*), and a smaller abundance of fragments of dicotylenous (broad leaf, mostly deciduous) trees and shrubs, as well as possible food fragments. Based on these results we would suggest that a cold and humid spruce woodland existed in the vicinity of the site during the occupation phase. Some cold resistant deciduous broad leaf trees/shrubs (such as willow, silver birch, mountain ash) could have grown in such an environment as well. However, on the basis of the shape and context of the hearth we also recognized during the excavation that it cannot be entirely excluded that only a single spruce log burnt in the feature. This well preserved feature could have resulted in an over-representation of the species (*Picea abies*) in the archeobotanical assemblage, adding a cautionary note to the paleoenvironmental reconstruction (Fig. 4).

The overlaying stratigraphic level above the cultural layer contained burnt charcoal, and was radiocarbon dated to 22,480 ± 120 B.P. (Beta 159856). The date and the nature of the sedimentation suggest mild Tursac oscillation geochronology. This layer (corresponding to Bánesz' Paleolithic phase II) was represented by charcoal sam-

ples of deciduous trees, both above and below the artifacts bearing layer. The ratio between deciduous and coniferous fragments was 5:1, suggesting a warmer and/or more humid climate.

The additional cultural level with numerous lithic artifacts that we sampled for archeobotanical remains was located in excavation unit 5, located 75 m from the top on the northern slope of the hill. Here level 2, only 22 cm below the

Fig. 4. Cejkov 2001, hearth recovery in unit 1, layer 5

plough zone, contained oak (*Quercus*), rose (*Rosa*), deciduous, coniferous, and indeterminate charcoal, as well as potential food remains. The suggested paleoenvironment appears to have been warmer open mixed deciduous (oak) woodland, with possible pioneer conifers (e.g., pine, juniper) growing in extreme locations such as slopes or marshes. However, soil analysis of this excavation unit suggested a clear postdepositional soil movement, cryoturbation and the layers were visibly disturbed through anthropogenic activities, leading us to a much more skeptical view of the paleoenvironmental reconstruction from this unit.

Consequently, we feel confident about establishing a securely dated Gravettian occupation of eastern Slovakia at the locality of Cejkov on the basis of soil, archeobotanical, and archaeological materials from excavation unit 1. (The few associated animal bones were too fragile and too small for identification.) This occupation occurred in a cold, humid spruce woodland setting, dated to 23–25 Kyr.

All dates were AMS ^{14}C dates based on charcoal samples:

23,440 ± 120 B.P. (Beta 159853)
23,820 ± 40 B.P. (Beta 159852)
24,130 ± 130 B.P. (Beta 159855)
24,240 ± 120 B.P. (Beta 159854)
24,800 ± 110 B.P. (Beta 159851)

This article places Cejkov within a larger central and east European context. A much more detailed account of Cejkov with site maps, illustrations of site profiles, recovered lithic artifacts, and a discussion of typology, and raw materials were published elsewhere, and we refer interested readers to that publication (Kaminská and Tomášková, 2004).

ARCHAEOLOGICAL MATERIALS

The entire surface collection from the southern slope of the Tokaj Hill consisted of 377 typologically defined Paleolithic artifacts. Most numerous were burins, such as an obsidian dihedral lateral burin, a dihedral burin on a tanged retouched limnic quartzite blade, and a multiple dihedral burin made on opal. The majority of the collected artifacts were flakes, 318 of them made on obsidian, six on limnic quartzite, three on chert, two on opal, and one on menilithic flint (Tables 2–3).

The upper layers of the excavation units 1–5/2001 contained mostly flakes, 43 of them were made on obsidian and one on limnic quartzite, in

Table 2

Cejkov: Lithic collection, basic typology

Unit & Layer	Cores	Blades	Micro-blades	Flakes	Burin spalls	Retouched tools	Total
Surface Collections		35	4	330	1	7	377
S1-1.layer	3	2		44			49
S1-2.layer		1		5			6
S1-5.layer	2	4		18			24
S2-1.layer	6	9		52		1	68
S2-2.layer		1		5			6
S2-3.layer			1	9			10
S3-1.layer		3	1	9		1	14
S4-1.layer				24	1	1	26
S4-2.layer				6			6
S4-6.layer				1			1
S5		2		15		13	30
Total	**11**	**57**	**6**	**518**	**2**	**23**	**617**

Table 3

Cejkov: Raw materials by excavation unit and layer

Unit & Layer	Obsidian	Limnic-quarzite	Quartz-itic sand-stone	Radio-larite	Opal	Brown chert	Menilithic chert	Chert	Flint
Surface	365	6			2		1	3	
S1-1.layer	48	1							
S1-2.layer	6								
S1-5.layer	13	10	1						
S2-1.layer	57	1	5	2					3
S2-2.layer	5		1						
S2-3.layer	4	1		1	4				
S3-1.layer	12	1			1				
S4-1.layer	21		3					2	
S4-2.layer	4		2						
S4-6.layer	1								
S5	1	13		5		6		3	2
Total	**537**	**33**	**12**	**8**	**7**	**6**	**1**	**8**	**5**

Table 4

Cejkov: Lithic industry, typology by unit and layer

Stone tools	Unit 2	Unit 3	Unit 4	Unit 5		Surface collections	Total
	Layer 1	Layer 1	Layer 1	Layer 2	Layer 3		
Blade scraper				1	1		2
Scraper-burin				3			3
Drill						1	1
Dihedral burin				1		2	3
Bipolar dihedral burin				1			1
Lateral burin	1						1
Multiple burin		1					1
Burin on a retouched blade						1	1
Retouched blade			1	2		2	5
Stemmed scraper				2			2
Stemmed burin				1			1
Chisel						1	1
Backed microblade				1			1
Total	**1**	**1**	**1**	**12**	**1**	**7**	**23**

Table 5

Cejkov: Lithic industry, typology by raw material

Stone tools	Obsidian	Limnic quartzite	Quartzitic sandstone	Opal	Brown chert	Chert	Flint
Blade scraper		1				1	
Scraper-burin					3		
Drill	1						
Dihedral burin	1	1		1			
Bipolar dihedral burin		1					
Lateral burin							1
Multiple Burin				1			
Burin on a retouched blade		1					
Retouched blade	2		1		1	1	
Stemmed scraper		2					
Stemmed burin		1					
Chisel	1						
Backed microblade		1					
Total	**5**	**8**	**1**	**2**	**4**	**2**	**1**

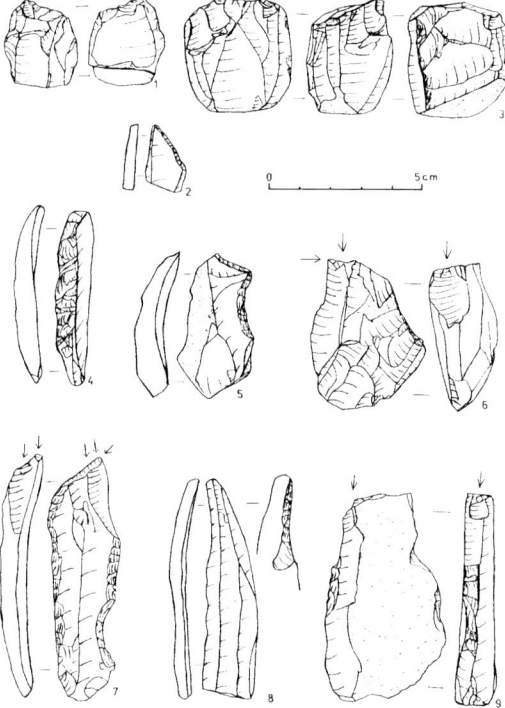

Fig. 5.   Cejkov 2001, surface collection, lithic artifacts

addition to three obsidian cores. The obsidian from the top two layers was grayish black with fluid texture, a type that is most common in the Zemplín area of eastern Slovakia. Limnic quartzite is very common at Cejkov I, appearing in all layers in numerous color variants. Limnic quartzite sources are known in eastern Slovakia (Kaminská, 1991:20) but the raw material used in Cejkov I resembles limnic quartzites from northeastern Hungary. Similarly, the nontransparent black obsidian, found alongside the grayish black variety, is most likely from the Hungarian sources (Williams-Thorpe *et al.*, 1984). The brown chert, used in the majority of the stone artifacts, is known from the central Ondava river valley, concentrated near Nižný Hrabovec the location of our initial survey (Tables 4–5).

The lithic industry from layer 5, the only stratigraphically secure and dated layer in excavation unit 1, consisted of cores, flakes and blades. Raw materials were represented by nontransparent black obsidian, quartzitic sandstone, and limnic quartzite. We conclude that the settlement in the Ondava river valley in eastern Slovakia represents a well established presence of Late Gravettian

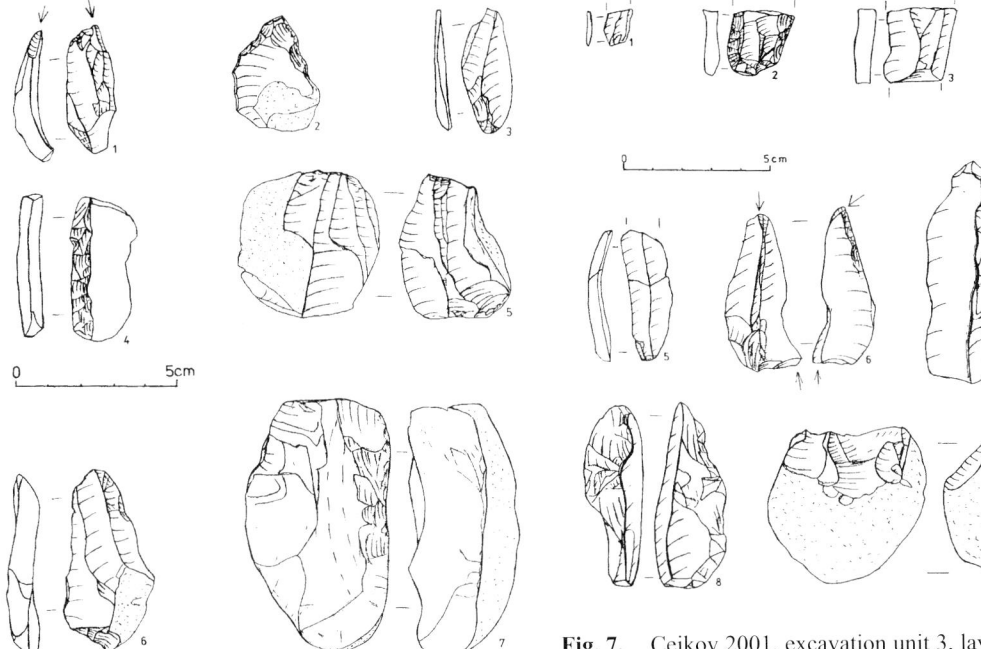

Fig. 6. Cejkov 2001, excavation unit 2, layer 1, lithic artifacts

Fig. 7. Cejkov 2001, excavation unit 3, layer 1 (1, 3, 6), unit 4, layer 1 (2, 4), and unit 1 layer 5 (5, 7, 8, 9)

groups in the area. The archaeological materials suggest mobility and/or contacts within the region, as well as between adjacent regions, leading us to a wider comparison of contemporaneous sites in central and eastern Europe (Figs. 4–9).

CONTEMPORANEOUS LATE GRAVETTIAN SITES IN CENTRAL AND EASTERN EUROPE

The initial research interest in this project was the nature and extent of social interactions between Gravettian groups in central and eastern Europe, as a move towards Paleolithic social archaeology. Our initial investigation of the sources of raw materials from Paleolithic collections in eastern Slovakia suggested regional as well as long distances sources, indicating social contacts and interactions and/or travel in eastern, northern, and southern directions. To expand this horizon, and evaluate the possibility of intra- and inter-regional contacts, we have collected contemporaneous dates with Cejkov from other sites in central and eastern Europe, working with a time

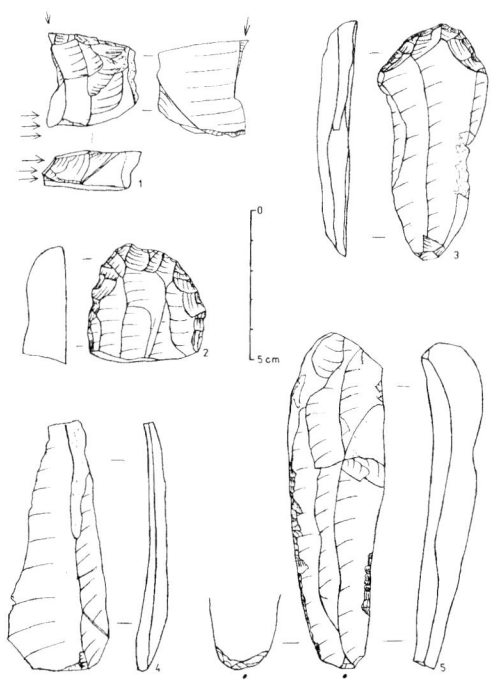

Fig. 8. Cejkov 2001, excavation unit 5, lithic artifacts

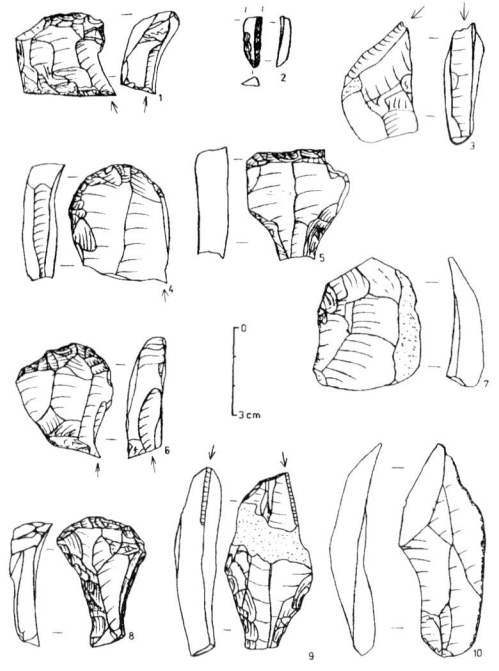

Fig. 9. Cejkov 2001, excavation unit 5, lithic artifacts

frame of 25–22 Kyr B.P. While this time frame is still quite broad for a discussion of occupational contemporaneity, it serves to narrow down the list of sites that could be viewed as geochronologically contemporaneous by excluding other sites that are most likely not overlapping in time.

In debates of Paleolithic foraging groups strict contemporaneity is a complex, if not an outright impossible, concept. Most progress has been made in recent years in lithic and faunal studies that focused on the organization of technology, particularly in re-fitting studies (e.g., Audouze and Enloe, 1997; Conard and Adler, 1997; Dibble *et al.*, 1997; Hoffman and Enloe, 1992). These studies mainly address taphonomy and postdepositional issues within sites and their immediate surroundings. Regional and inter-regional contemporaneity is equally if not more complex and most of the time is based on typological similarities that are correlated with geochronology and depositional history. With the growing number of radiocarbon dates and calibration of older dates, it is increasingly possible and justifiable to address contemporaneity between regions on the basis of dating, so as to suggest models for possible social

interactions. It is to this end that we present the following data set of potential contemporaneous sites within central and eastern Europe.

In considering the possible social landscape of late Upper Paleolithic central and eastern Europe, we present those sites for which published ^{14}C dates are available, rather than relying on suggested date ranges based on typology of recovered archaeological materials. We include only sites with dates that have confirmed laboratory numbers, although we are aware of the need for a certain degree of caution if only a single date is available. Whenever the information is available, we also include the type of dated material (information that is still far too scarce) to allow for the possibility of evaluating the reliability of the date and considering the potential contaminants. The data included covers both central and eastern Europe in order to suggest possible contacts, exchanges and/or social interactions. This is not to exclude the possibility of contacts between groups located in western and southern Europe and those inhabiting central and eastern Europe, but rather highlighting areas that have not received as much attention in previous discussions. The distances considered in this essay range from adjacent sites 2–5 km apart (e.g., Dolní Věstonice, Pavlov, Milovice), to those separated by moderate distances under 100 km (e.g., Alberndorf and Willendorf, Alberndorf and Dolní Věstonice, or Mitoc Malu Galben and Korpatch), and finally to those separated by longer distances over 100 kms (e.g., Cejkov and Krakow-Spadzista, which are 224 km apart; Tables 6–7).

SIMILARITIES AND DIFFERENCES IN SETTLEMENT PATTERNS IN CENRAL AND EASTERN EUROPE

The currently best known Upper Paleolithic locations in Germany are cave sites, predominantly in the south, along the Danube and its tributaries, such as Bockstein Torle, Obere Klause, or Hohle Fels (see Fig. 1). However open air sites are becoming better known in southern Germany, such as Salching and Steinacker, and the Rhineland, such as Rhens, Wildscheuer, Mainz-Linsenberg, and Spredlingen (Scheer, 2000). Until recently the greatest focus in this area has been on Aurignacian and Magdalenian

Table 6

Central and east European contemporaneous sites 25-22 Kyr B.P.

#	Country and site	Date	Lab number	Sample material	Reference
	Germany				
1	Kniegrotte	25,340 ± 440	OxA 4847		Street & Terberger, 2000
2	Bockstein Torle VI	23,440 ± 290	H 4058-3526		Street & Terberger, 2000
3	Obere Klause	24,680 ± 360	OxA 5721		Street & Terberger, 2000
4	Geissenklosterle Ir	24,360 ± 380	OxA 5157		Street & Terberger, 2000
	Geissenklosterle Ia	23,625 ± 290	H 5117-4568		Street & Terberger, 2000
5	Hohle Fels IIb	23,100 ± 70	Pta 2746		Street & Terberger, 2000
6	Vogelherd IV-V	23,860 ± 190	GrN 6583		Street & Terberger, 2000
	Vogelherd V/6	23,020 ± 400	H 4055-3209		Street & Terberger, 2000
	Austria				
7	Alberndorf	25,350 ± 450	VRI 1536	mammoth bone	Trnka, 2004
		25 400 ± 260	ETH 13040	bone (AMS)	Trnka, 2004
		23,170 ± 230	ETH 13041	bone (AMS)	Trnka, 2004
		20,500 ± 1,400	VRI 1272	bone	Trnka, 2004
8	Grub/Kranawetberg	24,830 ± 230	GrA 9066		Antl & Fladerer, 2004
		24,930 ± 240	GrA 9065		Antl & Fladerer, 2004
		24,620 ± 230	GrA 9063		Antl & Fladerer, 2004
9	Willendorf II, layer 8	25,400 ± 170	GrN 21690	bone	Haesaerts, 1996
	Willendorf II, layer 8	25,230 ± 320	GrN 17801	charcoal	Haesaerts, 1996
	Willendorf II, layer 8	24,710 ± 180	GrA 894	charcoal	Haesaerts, 1996
	Willendorf II, above 8	23,200 ± 140	GrA 893	charcoal	Haesaerts, 1996
	Willendorf II, above 8	23,400 ± 120	GrA 493	charcoal	Haesaerts, 1996
	Willendorf II, above 8	23,670 ± 120	GrA 494	charcoal	Haesaerts, 1996
	Willendorf II, layer 9	23,860 ± 270	GrN 21898	bone	Haesaerts, 1996
	Willendorf II, layer 9	24,370 ± 290	GrN 22208	bone	Haesaerts, 1996
	Willendorf II, layer 9	24,910 ± 150	GrA 5006	bone	Haesaerts, 1996
	Czech & Slovak Rep.				
10	Brno 2	23,680 ± 200	OxA		Oliva, 2000
11	Dolni Vestonice II	23,540 ± 180	GrA 19498		Svoboda, 2004
	Dolni Vestonice II-2	24,560 ± 660-610	GrN 20329	charcoal	Van der Plicht, 1997
	Dolni Vestonice III	25,160 ± 170	GrN 22304	charcoal	Van der Plicht, 1997
	Dolni Vestonice III	25,840 ± 290	GrN 22305	charcoal	Van der Plicht, 1997
	Dolni Vestonice III unit 2	25,530 ± 110	GrA 192	charcoal	Van der Plicht, 1997
	Dolni Vestonice IV 87-1	25,950 ± 630	GrN 18189	charcoal	Van der Plicht, 1997
	Dolni Vestonice IV 25d	25,740 ± 210	GrN 15277	charcoal	Van der Plicht, 1997
	Dolni Vestonice IV/E3	23,370 ± 160	GrA 891	charcoal	Van der Plicht, 1997
12	Pavlov I	25,020 ± 150	GrN 1325	charcoal	Svoboda, 2000
13	Predmosti II	25,040 ± 320	GrN 1325		Svoboda, 2000

Table 6 continued
Central and east European contemporaneous sites 25-22 Kyr B.P.

#	Country and site	Date	Lab numer	Sample material	Reference
14	Milovice	22,900 ± 490	ISGS 1690		Oliva, 1989
		25,200 ± 280	GrN 14824		Oliva, 1989
		22,080 ± 530	ISGS 1901		Oliva, 1989
		22,100 ± 1,100	GrN 14825		Oliva, 1989
15	Petrkovice	23,370 ± 160	GrA 891		Svoboda, 2000
		20,790 ± 270	GrN 19540		Svoboda, 2000
16	Moravany Lopata	24,100 ± 800	Gd 10	bone	Pazdur, 1998
		21,400 ± 610	Gd 9	bone	Pazdur, 1998
17	Nitra Cerman	22,860 ± 400	GrN 2449		Barta, 1987
18	Cejkov	24,800 ± 110	Beta 159851	charcoal	
		23,820 ± 40	Beta 159852	charcoal	
		23,440 ± 120	Beta 159853	charcoal	
		24,130 ± 130	Beta 159855	charcoal	
	Poland				
19	Krakow Spadzista	23,040 ± 170	GrN 6636	carbonized bone	Wojtal, 2004
		23,020 ± 180	Poz 242	mammoth collagen	Wojtal, 2004
		23,750 ± 140	Poz 1248	mammoth collagen	Wojtal, 2004
		23,770 ± 160	Poz 1251	mammoth collagen	Wojtal, 2004
		23,980 ± 280	Poz 225	mammoth collagen	Wojtal, 2004
		24,000 ± 300	Poz 268	mammoth collagen	Wojtal, 2004
	Balkans (Adriatic)				
20	Sandalija II, layer E	23,540 ± 180	GrN 5013		
	Romania				
21	Mitoc Malu Galben	23,650 ± 400	OxA 1779	bone	ORAU date list 11
		24,650 ± 450	OxA 1780	bone	
		24,800 ± 430	OxA 2033	bone	
	Ukraine, Moldova & Russia				
22	Korpatch	25,250 ± 300	GrN 9758		Anikovitch, 1992
23	Korolevo 1, layer 1a	25,700 ± 400	Gro 2773		Anikovitch, 1992
24	Molodova V, layer 7	23,700 ± 320	GIN 10		Kozlowski, 1984
		23,000 ± 800	MO 11		Kozlowski, 1984
25	Kostenki 1, layer 1	21,300 ± 400	GIN 2534		Kozlowski, 1984
		22,300 ± 230	GIN 1870		Iakovleva, 2000
		22,800 ± 200	GIN 2530		Iakovleva, 2000
		23,000 ± 500	GIN 2528		Iakovleva, 2000
		23,500 ± 200	GIN 2527		Iakovleva, 2000
	Kostenki 11, layer 2	21,800 ± 200	GIN 2531		Kozlowski, 1984
	Kostenki 21, layer 3	22,270 ± 150	GrN 7363		Kozlowski, 1984

Table 6 continued
Central and east European contemporaneous sites 25-22 Kyr B.P.

#	Country and site	Date	Lab number	Sample material	Reference
26	Sungir	24,430 ± 400	Gro 5446		Anikovich, 1992
		25,500 ± 500	Gro 5425		Anikovich, 1992
27	Avdeevo	22,400 ± 600	GIN 1969		
		22,200 ± 700	GIN 1970		
28	Khotilevo 2	23,660 ± 270	LU 359		
		24,960 ± 400	IGAN 73		
	Siberia				
29	Sagaidak	21,240 ± 200	LE 1602A		Leonova, 1994
30	Anui II, layer 4	21,500 ± 585	IGAN 1431		
	Anui II, layer 8	22,610 ± 140	SOAN 2862		
	Anui II, layer 8	24,205 ± 420	SOAN 3006		Vasilev, 2000
31	Sabanikha	22,930 ± 480	LE 3611	charcoal	Vasilev, 2000
		22,930 ± 350	LE 4701	charcoal	Vasilev, 2000
32	Kurtak IV, layer 2	24,890 ± 670	LE 3357	bone	Vasilev, 2000
		24,800 ± 400	GIN 5350	charcoal	Vasilev, 2000
		24,170 ± 230	LE 3351	charcoal	Vasilev, 2000
		24,000 ± 2,950	LE 4156	bone	Vasilev, 2000
		23,800 ± 900	LE 4155	charcoal	Vasilev, 2000
		23,470 ± 200	LE 2833	charcoal	Vasilev, 2000
33	Kashtanka I, layer 1	24,805 ± 425	SOAN 2853	charcoal	Vasilev, 2000
	Kashtanka I, layer 1	23,830 ± 850	IGAN 1050		
	Kashtanka I, above 2	24,400 ± 1,500	IGAN 1048	charcoal	Vasilev, 2000
34	Igeteiskii Log 1, layer 6	24,400 ± 100	GIN 4327	bone	Vasilev, 2000
	Igeteiskii Log 1, layer 4	23,760 ± 1,100	SOAN 405	charcoal	Vasilev, 2000
		23,508 ± 250	LE 1592	charcoal	Vasilev, 2000
		21,260 ± 240	LE 1590	charcoal	Vasilev, 2000
35	Ust'Kova, layer 5	23,920 ± 310	KRIL 381	charcoal	Vasilev, 2000
36	Masterov Kliuch, layer 4	24,360 ± 270	AA 8888	bone	Vasilev, 2000
37	Arta II, layer 3	23,200 ± 2,000	LE 2967	charcoal	Vasilev, 2000
38	Shestakovo, layer 22	22,240 ± 185	SOAN 3612		Vasilev et al., 2003
	layer 22	22,250 ± 280	SOAN 4177		
	layer 22	22,750 ± 180	GrA 15880		
	layer 22	23,330 ± 110	GrA 13235		
	layer 19	23,250 ± 110	GrA 13233		
	layer 19	23,290 ± 200	AA 35322		
	layer 19	22,340 ± 180	GrA 13240		
	layer 19	24,360 ± 150	GrA 10935		
	layer 24	24,590 ± 110	GrA 13239		
	layer 24	25,660 ± 200	GrA 13238		

Table 7

Central and east European late Gravettian locations

#	Site	Location	Altitude (m)	Description
1	Kniegrotte	Lat. 50°42'N Lon 11°39'E	371	Cave, Thuringia
2	Bockstein Torle VI	Lat. 48°44'30N Lon 10°56'47E		Cave, S Germany
3	Obere Klause	Lat. 48°55'53N Lon 12°8'E	410	Cave, Bavaria
4	Geissenklosterle Ir	Lat. 48°23'53N Lon 9°46'39"E		Cave
5	Hohle Fels Iib	Lat. 48°22'50N Lon 9°43'57"E	550	Cave, Ach valley Danube tributary
6	Vogelherd IV-V	Lat 48°34'N Lon 10°12'E	502	Cave, Lone valley, Danube tributary
7	Alberndorf	Lat 48°42'N Lon 16°6'E	199	Open air
8	Grub/Kranawetberg	Lat 48°25'N Lon 16°50'E	141	Open air
9	Willendorf II,	Lat 48°19'N Lon 15°24'E	194	Open air, Danube valley
10	Brno 2	Lat 49°12'N Lon 16°38' E	215	Open air
11	Dolni Vestonice I	Lat 48°53'N Lon 16°39'E	284	Open air, river valley
12	Pavlov I	Lat 48°52'N Lon 16°40'E	200	Open air
13	Predmosti II	Lat 49°28'N Lon 17°27'E	233	Open air
14	Milovice	Lat 48°51'N Lon 16°42'E	200	Open air
15	Petrkovice	Lat 49°33'N Lon 17°57'E	520	Open air
16	Moravany Lopata	Lat 48°36'N Lon 17°52'E	325	Open air, Vah valley
17	Nitra Cerman	Lat 48°19'N Lon 18°5'E	248	Open air
18	Cejkov	Lat 48°28'N Lon 21°46'E	177	Open air, Ondava valley
19	Krakow Spadzista	Lat 50°5'N Lon 19°55'E	232	Open air
20	Sandalija II, layer E	Lat 44°53'33N Lon 13°51'E	16	Adriatic coast
21	Mitoc Malu Galben	Lat 47°43'N Lon 26°41'E	153	Prut river valley
22	Korpatch	Lat 48°4'10N Lon 27°8'18E	161	Open air
23	Korolevo 1	Lat 48°9'N Lon 23°8'E	136	Open air
24	Molodova V,	Lat 48°33'N Lon 27°5'E	198	Open air, Dnestr river valley
25	Sagaidak	Lat 48°2'N Lon 32°45'E	170	Open air, Bug river
26	Kostenki 1	Lat 51°23'33N Lon 39°3'14E	83	Open air
27	Sungir	Lat. 56°11'N Lon. 40°30'E	101	Open air near Vladimir
28	Avdeevo	Lat 51°41'24N Lon 35°47'54E	159	Kursk region open air
29	Khotilevo 2	Lat 53°20'13N Lon 34°7'26E	160	Open air Middle Desna river bank

settlements, with the assumption that Gravettian ones were either rare or absent. However, research in the last decade has shown occupation during the Gravettian as well (see e.g., Hahn, 2000; Scheer, 1993, 2000; Street and Terberger, 2000) encouraging exploration of possible contacts between regions. The main difference between this region and more eastern sites is the location of Gravettian sites in caves, an uncommon settlement pattern in the rest of central and eastern Europe. Raw material acquisition in western central Europe also appears more localized (Féblot-Augustins, 1993, 1997; Scheer, 1993, 2000), or confined to western Danube valley and its tributaries, with the river valley serving as the main transportation route. However, Scheer also documents communication between groups that occupied Hohle Fehls, Geissenklosterle and the Black

Table 8

Late Gravettian Siberian site locations

#	Site	Location
30	Anui II	Lat 51° 39' N Long 85° 06' E
31	Sabanikha	Lat. 54° 58' N Long 91° 7' E
32	Kurtak IV	Lat. 55° 17' N Long 91° 58' E
33	Kashtanka I	Lat. 55° 15' N Long 91° 55' E
34	Igeteiskii Log I	Lat. 53° 58' N Long 103° 42' E
35	Ust'Kova	Lat. 58° 3' N Long 100° 33' E
36	Masterov Kliuch	Lat. 50° 43' N Long 110° E
37	Arta II	Lat. 51° 25' N Long 112° 40' E
38	Shestakovo	Lat. 56° 30' N Long 88° 35' E

Forest region to the west (Scheer, 2000:263). Contacts between southern Germany and upper Rhine valley are also well documented on the basis of raw material sourcing, and should provide a solid ground for further exploration of social networks and exchanges (Hahn, 2000; Scheer, 2000).

The majority of sites in Austria, Czech and Slovak Republics display similar settlement pattern of open air sites in slight elevations above river valleys. Despite this similarity the Gravettian locations also display interesting differences in occupational duration, raw material acquisition, and possibly social networks (for detailed studies see entries in Roebroeks *et al.*, 2000; Svoboda and Sedláčková, 2004). The proximity between eastern Slovakia and the Ukraine – 106 km between Cejkov and Korolevo, on one hand, and sites in Moldova and Romania – 52 km between Mitoc Malu Galben and Korpatch, is a topic that

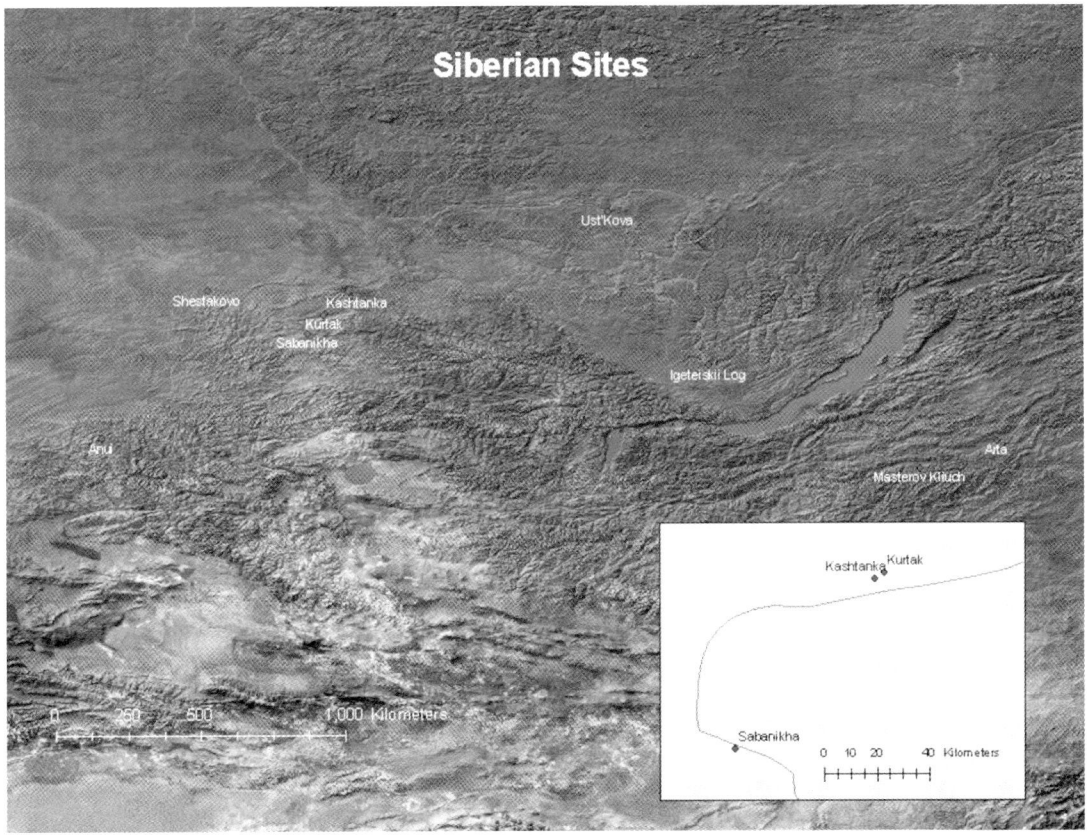

Fig. 10. Distribution of Siberian Late Gravettian sites (22–25 Kyr)

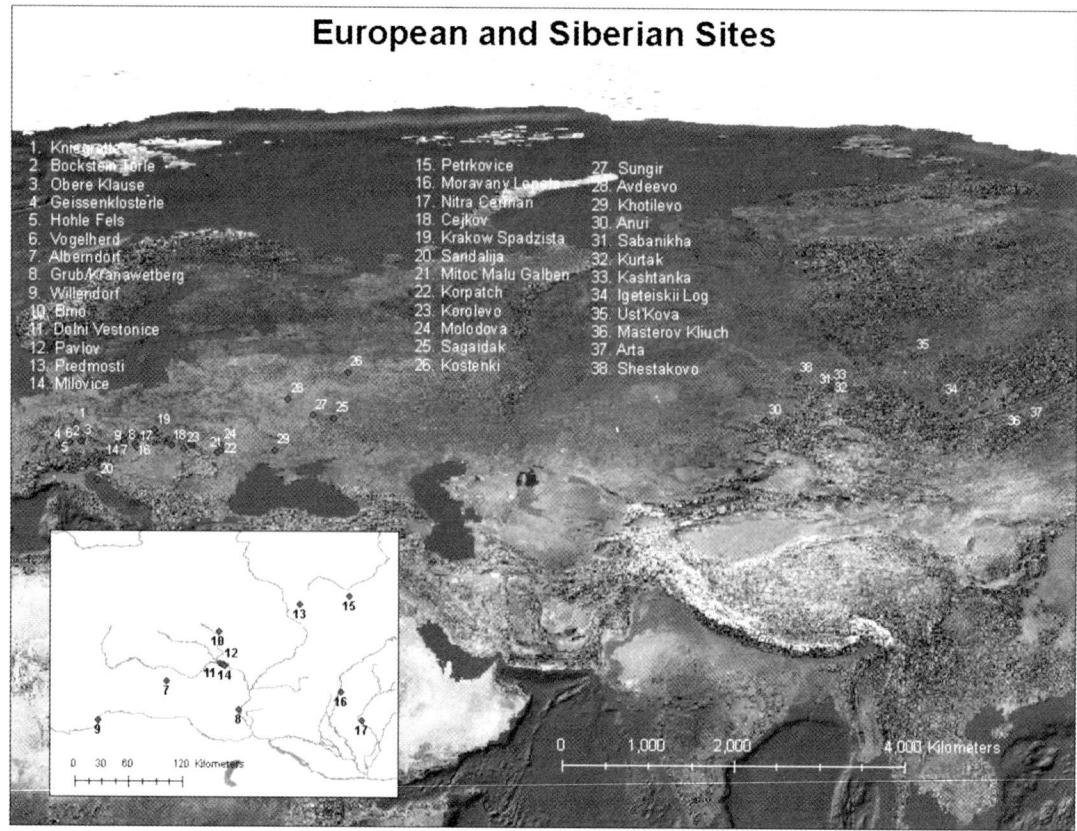

Fig. 11. Distribution of Central, East European and Siberian Late Gravettian sites (22–25 Kyr)

has received very little attention (for an exception see Haesaerts *et al.*, 2003), and should be explored further in the future. The interesting absence of sites on the map of late Gravettian settlements is posed by the Hungarian Plain and Poland (Fig. 1; for a discussion of Pleistocene settlements in the Polish Carpathians see Valde-Nowak, 1991). While Hungarian Upper Paleolithic is well established at this point with confirmed dates from Aurignacian sites, and early Gravettian sites, such as Bodrogkeresztúr-Henye ([14]C: 28,700 ± 3000 B.P., GXO 195; 26,318 ± 365 B.P., Deb. 2555), Megyaszó-Szelesteto ([14]C: 27,070 ± 680 B.P., Deb. 5372), Püspökhatvan-Diós Öregszolo ([14]C: 27,700 ± 300, Deb. 1901), Hont-Parassa III/Orgonás ([14]C: 27,350 ± 610, Deb. 5027) (Dobosi, 2000b), the next reliably dated time period appears only after 20 thousand years before present, such as Mogyorosbanya ([14]C: 19,930 ± 300 B.P., Deb 1169) (Dobosi, 2000b:232). The current paucity of dates between 25–20 Kyr B.P. in this region merits further exploration, particularly considering its proximity to eastern Slovakia where we now have evidence of settlements in this time range, along with the presence of raw materials from the Hungarian Plain.

Eastern Europe as presented here includes parts of present-day Russia continuing eastward into Siberia. This landscape is dramatically different from western and central Europe, particularly in terms of climate, ecology, and history of the landscape. The scale of physical features is likewise different, starting from the vastness of the east European Plain. Stretching from the Arctic Ocean in the north to the Black sea in the south, this lowland encompasses mainly low elevations that are drier and cooler than any areas of central or eastern Europe. Understanding the history of this landscape is an important part of any effort to evaluate the archaeology and human occupation of adjacent regions. Consequently we include the Siberian Late Upper Paleolithic record as a significant reminder of the wealth of human occupation to the east of the Ural Mountains, and refer the reader to literature that focuses on the region in greater detail, and is increasingly becoming accessible to English speakers (e.g. Hoffecker, 1999, 2002; Vasil'ev, 2000; Vasil'ev *et al.*, 2003; Table 8; Fig. 10).

CONCLUSION

In this work we have described initial results of our survey and excavations in eastern Slovakia in 2000 and 2001. To better situate the site of Cejkov we have also reviewed comparable dates from known Paleolithic sites in surrounding regions, and provide a summary of the results in order to facilitate the larger task of reconstructing prehistoric patterns of settlement during the time period. The recent increase in the number of securely dated sites in central and eastern Europe also provides a basis for a discussion of a possible variation in human adaptation to a worsening or unstable climate in central Europe (Soffer and Gamble, 1990; Roebroeks *et al.*, 2000). The possibility of ecological niches that allowed either a continued occupation or periodic visits in the area is becoming increasingly accepted in Late Upper Paleolithic studies of Europe (Montet-White, 1994, Roebroeks *et al.*, 2000). Our results from eastern Slovakia fit well within such an interpretive framework, clearly indicating widespread human presence in the region at a point 23–25,000 B.P (Fig. 11).

Acknowledgements

The Cejkov project research was supported by an International Collaborative Grant awarded to Drs. Tomášková and Kaminská by the Wenner-Gren Foundation, and by a grant from the Leakey Foundation. The Texas Archeological Research Laboratory, University of Texas at Austin is gratefully acknowledged for its computers and software used for map generation. The authors are grateful to Dr. M. Pawlikowski, Krakow University, Poland for the raw material analysis, and to Dr. G. Trnka University of Vienna, Austria for making the results of the Alberndorf project available to us. Wren Fournier generously aided in the final preparation of the manuscript, and several anonymous reviewers provided helpful comments but all interpretations and possible errors remain solely our responsibility.

REFERENCES

ALLSWORTH-JONES P. 1994. Dating the Paleolithic in Eastern Europe. *Newsletter of the Center for the Archaeology of Central and Eastern Europe* 2, 9–10.

ANIKOVICH M. 1992. Early Upper Paleolithic industries of Eastern Europe. *Journal of World Prehistory* 6(2), 205–245.

ANTL W., FLEDERER F. A. 2004. Outlook to the East: The 25 ky BP Gravettian Grub Kanawetberg site (Lower Austria). In: J. Svoboda, L. Sedláčková (eds.) *The Gravettian along the Danube*. The Dolní Věstonice Studies, vol. 11, 116–130.

AUDOUZE F., ENLOE J. G.1997. High resolution archaeology at Verberie: Limits and interpretations. *World Archaeology* 29(2), 195–207.

BACHNER M., MATEICIUCOVÁ I., TRNKA G. 1996. Die Spätaurignacien-Station Alberndorf im Pulkautal, NÖ. In: Svoboda, J., P. Škrdla, E. W. Oches (eds.) *Paleolithic in the Middle Danube Region*. Archeologický ústav AV CR, Brno, 93–119.

BÁNESZ L. 1969, Gravettské súvrstvia s obsidiánovou a pazúrikovou industriou v Kašove a Cejkove. *Archeologické rozhledy* 21, 281–290.

BÁNESZ L. 1976. Prírodné prostredie, hospodárska základňa a materiálna kultúra Aurignacienu strednej Európy. *Slovenská Archaeologia* 24, 5–82.

BÁNESZ L. 1980. Počiatky mladšieho paleolitu na východnom Slovensku. *Historica Carpatica* 11, 185–217.

BÁNESZ L. 1989. Problems of the Upper Paleolithic in the north-western part of the Carpathian basin. *Anthropologie* 27/2–3, 245–249.

BÁNESZ L. 1990. Súčasná problematika paleolitu východného Slovenska a severovýchodnej časti Karpatskej kotliny. *Historica carpatica* 21, 9–19.

BÁNESZ L. 1996. Entdeckungen der Kunstobjekte im Paläolithikum der Ostslowakei. In: J. Svoboda, P. Škrdla, E. W. Oches (eds.) *Paleolithic in the Middle Danube region*. Archeologický ústav AV CR, Brno, 279–281.

BÁNESZ L., PIETA K. 1961. Výskum v Cejkove I v roku 1960. *Štúdijné zvesti AÚ SAV* 6, 5–30.

BÁNESZ L., ZUBKO P. 1992. Štiepane kamenné artefakty v okolí obce Nižný Hrabovec. In: *AVANS*, Nitra.

BÁRTA J. 1965. *Slovensko v Staršej a Strednej Dobe Kamennej*. Vydavate_stvo Slovenskej Akadémie Vied, Bratislava.

BARTON R. N. E., JACOBI R. M., STAPERT D., STREET M. J. 2003. The Late-glacial reoccupation of the British Isles and the Creswellian. *Journal of Quaternary Science* 18/7, 631–643.

BORZIAC I. A. 1997. The Upper Paleolithic Site of Ciuntu on the Middle Prut, Moldova: a multidisciplinary study and reinterpretation. *Proceedings of the Prehistoric Society* 63, 285–301.

CHERNYSH O. P. 1982. Mnogosloinaia paleoliticheskaia stoyanka Molodova I. In: G. I. Goretskii, I. K. Ivanova (eds.) *Molodova I: Unikalnoe Musterskoe Poselenie na Srednem Dnestre.* Nauka, Moskva, 6–102.

CONARD N. J., ADLER D. S. 1997. Lithic reduction and hominid behavior in the Middle Paleolithic of the Rhineland. *Journal of Anthropological Research* 53, 147–175.

DIBBLE H., CHASE P., MCPHERRON S., TUFFREAU A. 1997. Testing the Reality of a "Living Floor" with Archaeological Data. *American Antiquity* 62(4), 629–651.

DOBOSI V. T. 2000a. Interior parts of the Carpathian Basin between 30,000 and 20,000 bp. In: W. Roebroeks, M. Mussi, J. Svoboda, K. Fennema (eds.) *Hunters of the Golden Age.* University of Leiden Press, Leiden, 231–239.

DOBOSI V. T. (ed.). 2000b. *Bodrogkeresztúr-Henye (NE-Hungary). Upper Palaeolithic Site.* Budapest.

FÉBLOT-AUGUSTINS J. 1993. Mobility strategies in the late Middle Paleolithic of Central Europe and Western Europe: elements of stability and variability. *Journal of Anthropological Archaeology* 12, 211–265.

FÉBLOT-AUGUSTINS J. 1997. Middle and Upper Paleolithic raw material transfers in Western and Central Europe: Assessing the pace of change. *Journal of Middle Atlantic Archaeology* 13, 57–90.

HAESAERTS P., DAMBLON F., BACHNER M., TRNKA G. 1996. Revised stratigraphy and chronology of the Willendorf II sequence, Lower Austria. *Archaeologia Austriaca* 80, 25–42.

HAESAERTS P., BORZIAK I., CHIRICA V., DAMBLON F., KOULAKOVSKA L., VAN DER PLICHT J. 2003. The East Carpathian loess record: a reference for the Middle and Late Pleniglacial stratigraphy in Central Europe. *Quaternaire* 14/3, 163–188.

HAESAERTS P., BORZIAK I., CHIRICA V., DAMBLON F., KOULAKOVSKA L. 2004. Cadre stratigraphique et chronologique du Gravettien en Europe Central. In: J. Svoboda, L. Sedláčková (eds.) *The Gravettian along the Danube.* The Dolní Věstonice Studies, vol. 11, 33–56.

HAHN J. 2000. The Gravettian in Southwest Germany – environment and economy. In: W. Roebroeks, M. Mussi, J. Svoboda, K. Fennema (eds.) *Hunters of the Golden Age.* University of Leiden Press, Leiden, 249–256.

HARČÁR J., KAMINSKÁ L., KAZIOR B., KACZANOWSKA M., KOZLOWSKI J. K., NOWAK M., PAWLIKOWSKI M., VIZDAL M. 1995/96. Lithic raw materials from the Slanské Mountains, Eastern Slovakia. *Acta Archaeologica Carpathica* 33, 5–23.

HOFFECKER J. 1999. Neanderthals and modern humans in Eastern Europe. *Evolutionary Anthropology* 7, 129–141.

HOFFECKER J. 2002. *Desolate Landscapes: Ice-Age Settlements in Eastern Europe.* New Brunswick: Rutgers University Press.

HOFFMAN L., ENLOE J. (eds.). 1992. *Piecing Together the Past: Applications of Refitting Studies in Archaeology.* B.A.R. International Series 578.

HROMADA J., KOZLOWSKI J. (eds.). 1995. *Complex of Upper Paleolithic Sites near Moravany, Western Slovakia,* vol. 1., Moravany-Zakovska. Jagellonian University Press, Kraków.

IAKOVLEVA L. 2000. The Gravettian art of Eastern Europe as exemplified in the figurative art of Kostenki 1. In: W. Roebroeks, M. Mussi, J. Svoboda, K. Fennema (eds.) *Hunters of the Golden Age.* University of Leiden Press, Leiden, 125–134.

KAMINSKÁ L. 1991. Význam surovinovej základne pre mladopaleolitickú spoločnost vo východokarpatskej oblasti. *Slovenská Archeologia* 39, 7–58.

KAMINSKÁ L., TOMÁŠKOVÁ S. 2004. Time and space systematics of Gravettian finds from Cejkov 1. In: J. Svoboda, L. Sedláčková (eds.) *The Gravettian along the Danube.* The Dolní Věstonice Studies, vol. 11, 186–216.

KOZLOWSKI J. K. 1986. The Gravettian in Central and Eastern Europe. *Advances in World Archaeology* 5, 131–200.

KOZLOWSKI J. K. (ed.). 1998. *Complex of Upper Paleolithic Sites near Moravany, Western Slovakia,* vol. 2, Moravany-Lopata. Jagellonian University Press, Kraków.

LEONOVA N. 1994. The Upper Paleolithic of the Russian steppe zone. *Journal of World Prehistory* 8(2), 169–210.

MONTET-WHITE A. 1988. Recent excavations at Grubgraben, a Gravettian site in Lower Austria. *Archaologisches Korrespondenzblatt* 18, 213–218.

MONTET-WHITE A. 1994. Alternative interpretations of the Late Upper Paleolithic in Central Europe. *Annual Reviews of Anthropology* 23, 483–508.

OTTE M., NOIRE P. 2004. Evolution du Gravettien au moyen Danube. In: J. Svoboda and L. Sedláčková (eds.) *The Gravettian along the Danube.* The Dolní Věstonice Studies, vol. 11, 8–32.

PAWLIKOWSKI M. 2000. Report submitted to the author.

ROEBROEKS W., MUSSI M., SVOBODA J., FEN-NEMA K. (eds.). 2000. *Hunters of the Golden Age*. University of Leiden Press, Leiden.

SCHEER A. 1993. The organization of lithic resource use during the Gravettian in Germany. In: H. Knecht, A. Pike-Tay, R. White (eds.) *Before Lascaux. The Complex Record of the Early Upper Paleolithic*. CRC Press, Ann Arbor, 193–210.

SCHEER A. 2000. The Gravettian in Southwest Germany: stylistic features, raw material resources and settlement patterns. In: W. Roebroeks, M. Mussi, J. Svoboda, K. Fennema (eds.) *Hunters of the Golden Age*. University of Leiden Press, Leiden, 257–270.

SOFFER O., GAMBLE C. (eds.). 1990. *The World at 18 000 BP*. Unwyn Hyman, London.

SOFFER O., PRASLOV N. D. (eds.). 1993. *From Kostenki to Clovis: Upper Paleolithic–Paleo-Indian Adaptations*. Plenum Press, New York.

STREET M., TERBERGER T. 2000. The German Upper Palaeolithic 35,000–15,000 bp. New dates and insights with emphasis on Rhineland. In: W. Roebroeks, M. Mussi, J. Svoboda, K. Fennema (eds.). *Hunters of the Golden Age*. University of Leiden Press, Leiden, 281–298.

SVOBODA J. 1991. *Paleolit Moravy a Slezska*. CSAV, Brno.

SVOBODA J., SEDLÁČKOVÁ L. (eds.). 2004. *The Gravettian along the Danube*. The Dolní Věstonice Studies, vol. 11.

SVOBODA J., SIMÁN K. 1989. Middle-Upper Paleo-lithic transition in southeastern central Europe. *Journal of World Prehistory*, 3(3), 283–322.

SVOBODA J., ŠKRDLA P., OCHES E. W. (eds.). 1996. *Paleolithic in the Middle Danube region*. Archeologický ústav AV CR, Brno.

TRINKAUS E., SVOBODA J., WEST D. L., SLADEK V., HILLSON S. W., DROZDOVA E., FISAKOVA M. 2000. Human remains from the Moravian Gravettian: Morphology and taphonomy of isolated elements from the Dolní Vestonice II site. *Journal of Archaeological Science*, 27, 1115–1132.

TRNKA G. 2004. personal communication.

VALDE-NOWAK P. 1991. Studies in Pleistocene settlements in the Polish Carpathians. *Antiquity* 65/248, 593–606.

VASIL'EV S., KUZMIN Y., ORLOVA L., DEMEN-TIEV V. 2002. Radiocarbon-based chronology of the Paleolithic in Siberia and its relevance to the peopling of the New World. *Radiocarbon*. 44/2, 503–530.

VERPOORTE A. 2004. Eastern Central Europe during the Pleniglacial, *Antiquity* 78(300), 257–266.

WILLIAMS O., NANDRIS J. 1977. The Hungarian and Slovak sources of archaeological obsidian: an interim report on further fieldwork, with a note on tektites. *Journal of Archaeological Science* 4, 207–219.

WILLIAMS-THORPE O., WARREN S. E., NANDRIS J. 1984. The distribution and provenance of archaeological obsidian in Central and Eastern Europe. *Journal of Archaeological Science* 11, 183–212.

Eurasian Prehistory, 2 (2): 33–56.

END OF THE PALEOLITHIC IN THE ARGOLID (GREECE): EXCAVATIONS IN CAVE 4 AND CAVE 7 IN THE KLISOURA GORGE

Margarita Koumouzelis[1], Janusz K. Kozłowski[2] and Małgorzata Kaczanowska[3]

[1] *Ephorate for Caves and Palaeoanthropology, 34b Ardittou, 11636 Athens, Greece*
[2] *Institute of Archaeology, Jagiellonian University, ul. Gołębia 11, 31007 Kraków, Poland;*
KOZLOWSK@argo.hist.uj.edu.pl
[3] *Archaeological Museum, ul. Senacka 3, 31002, Kraków, Poland*

Abstract

The results of the excavations in Caves 4 and 7 in Klisoura Gorge (Argolid, Greece) are discussed in this paper. Archaeological finds discovered in these caves fill chronological gaps noted during the excavations of Cave 1 between the Epigravettian settlement in layers IIa and IIb. In particular, the gap dated to about 16 Kyr B.P., and the Mesolithic layers 6 and 5a dated after 9 Kyr B.P. According to radiometric and geochemical data, the Late Paleolithic layers in Cave 7 correspond to the Alleröd interstadial, and in Cave 4 the Late Paleolithic settlement is contemporary with the Alleröd/Bölling oscillations. The industries from Cave 7 are characterized by non-geometric backed microliths and those from Cave 4 by angulated and convex backed microliths produced by the microburin technique. Generally the finds from Caves 7 and 4 can be compared with lithic phases IV–VI in Franchthi Cave in the Argolid. All dates are uncalibrated B.P.

INTRODUCTION

During the field surveys conducted in 1992 and 1993 in the Klisoura Gorge (Argolis, Greece), 35 caves were documented. One of the crucial zones for the Paleolithic/Mesolithic sequence in Greece is the Argolid plain and the surrounding hills where numerous caves are known although only a few have been excavated. A. Markovics conducted the first excavations of Ulbrich Cave in the Bay of Nafplion in 1928. The subsequent excavation was carried out by L. Reisch in the Kephalari Cave. Unfortunately, the results of these excavations have not been published, with the exception of some general remarks on the lithics (Hahn, 1984) and the the stratigraphy (Reisch, 1980). The primary reference for the Paleolithic/Mesolithic sequence in the Argolid remains Franchthi Cave, near Porto Heli. The lithic industries from this cave were carefully analysed and published by Perlès (1987, 1990). In 1992 and

1993, surveys and excavations found new Paleolithic/Mesolithic settlements on the eastern border of the Argolid plain, including 35 documented caves.

In some of these caves the sediments are fairly well preserved. In 1993, trenches were dug in Cave 4 and Cave 7 (Koumouzelis *et al.*, 1996). In Cave 1, block excavations were conducted in 1994–2003 (Koumouzelis *et al.*, 2001a, 2001b). In 1996, the results of the soundings in Cave 4 and Cave 7 were published as a brief preliminary report. These results deserve broader discussion and presentation as they fill chronological gaps between the Epigravettian settlement in Cave 1 (layers IIa–IIb) and the Mesolithic occupations (layers 5a and 6). It should be emphasized that the end of the Paleolithic in the Argolid is documented in few locations including Franchthi Cave "lithic phases" IV–VI near Porto Heli (Perlès, 1987), Ulbrich Cave layer V (Markovits, 1928; Tellenbach,

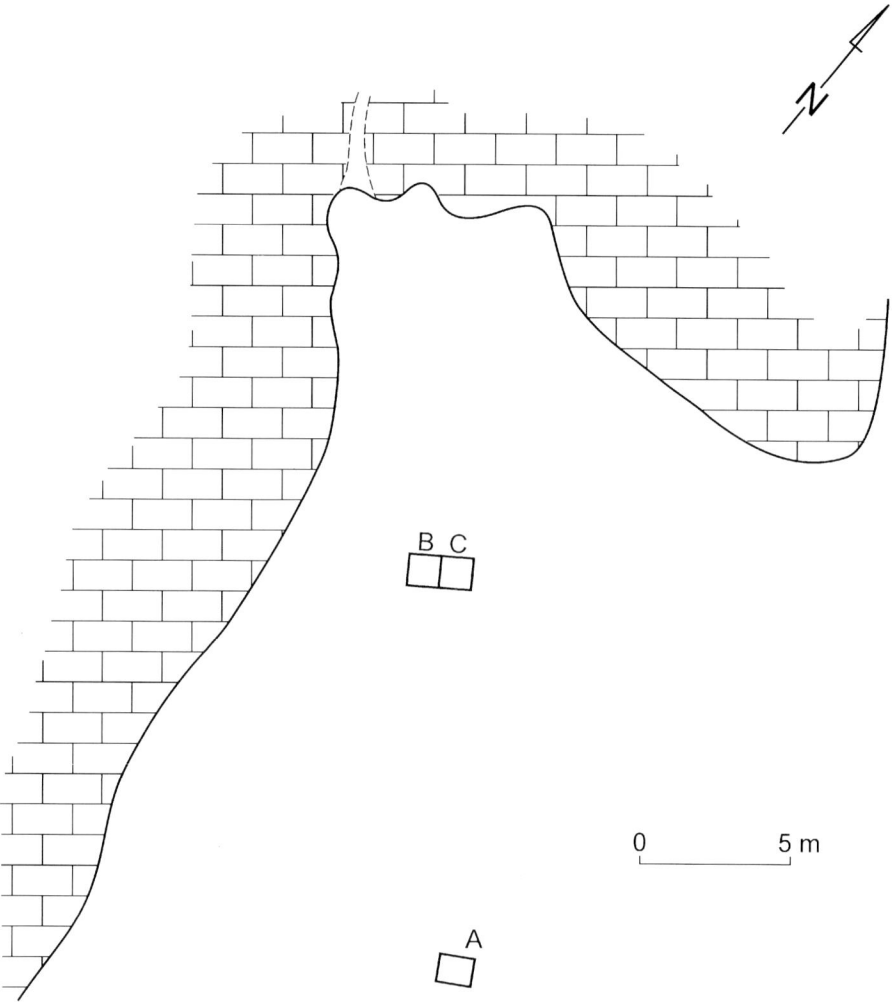

Fig. 1.   Klisoura Gorge, Cave 7. Map of the trenches

1983) situated in the neighborhood of Nafplion, and Zaimis Cave layers VIII–IX situated on the north side of the Saronic Gulf near Megara (Markovits, 1928; Tellenbach, 1983; Galanidou, 2003).

CAVE 7

Cave 7 is situated on the right bank of the Berbatiotis River, at an elevation of 30–35 m above the valley floor. The area of the interior of the cave measures ca. 30–40 m². Cave sediments were preserved in the places where they were covered by limestone breccia, and on the slope in front of the cave (Fig. 1).Three trenches measuring 1-x-1 m were dug. Trench A was excavated on the slope, and trench B and trench C were dug in front of Cave 7.

The stratigraphic sequence in trenches B and C consisted of three lithostratigraphical units (Fig. 2):

1) carbonate breccia with weakly weathered limestone rubble as a result of the formation of the calcitic layer before and after the sedimentation of clastic material;

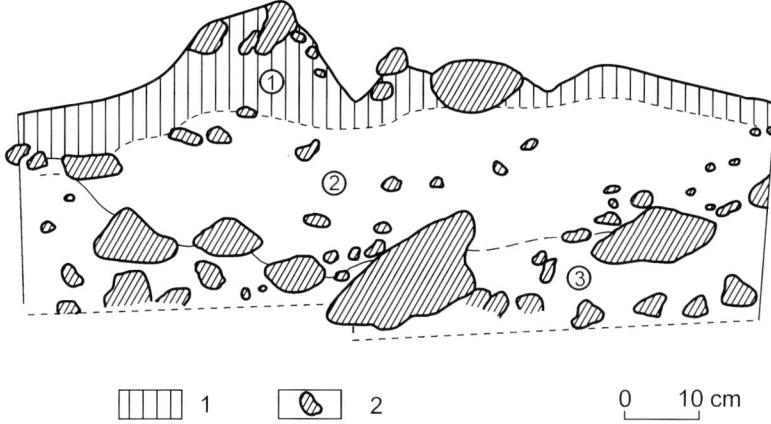

Fig. 2.   Klisoura Gorge, Cave 7. Northern section of trench B: 1) carbonate breccia; 2) limestone blocks

2) brown, clayey formation with fine, weathered limestone debris, partially cemented by calcium carbonate that formed efflorescence on the surface of the lithic artifacts;

3) fine-grained sediment, yellowish in color, containing a large amount of debris with fairly strongly weathered surfaces and rounded edges.

The layers described above are all dipping toward the southeast (at an angle of 20–25 degrees). The calcium carbonate from the dripstone underlying unit 1 has been radiocarbon dated to 12,500 ± 40 B.P. (Gd-3784), which after taking into account the reservoir effect should correspond to the date of ca. 10,850 B.P. (uncalibrated). Thus, the weakly weathered clastic material, forming unit 1 was probably deposited during Dryas III in the relatively cooler conditions that preceded and followed by the formation of dripstone when the activity of karstic waters increased.

Examination of layer 2 and layer 3 using X-ray diffraction patterns showed that these sediments were composed from calcite with an admixture of clay minerals, namely illite and poorly crystallized kaolinite (Fig. 3). The results of these examinations established that sediments 2 and 3 were the result of the crystallization of calcite mixed with terra rossa clay redeposited in warmer and wetter conditions than those during the formation of unit 1. This situation could correspond to the Alleröd Interstadial identified with the Xanthi warming phase registered in the pollen profiles in Greece (Bottema, 1974, 1994; Wijmstra, 1969; Turner and Sanchez-Goni, 1997).

ARCHAEOLOGY

Surface finds

Artifacts collected from the surface of Cave 7 belong to three groups that have been distinguished on typological bases:

1) Macroblades, possibly Neolithic, represented by:

– a bilaterally retouched blade from banded flint, violet in color (Fig. 4:1);

– a radiolarite blade with bilateral, slightly denticulated retouch and the tip obliquely truncated by steep retouch (Fig. 4:2); and

– a blade with unilateral and oblique transversal retouch, made from red flint (Fig. 4:3).

A proximal fragment of a blade with bilateral denticulated-notched retouch, made from radiolarite also belongs to this group.

2) Flakes, probably of Mesolithic age. The following artifacts made from local radiolarite belong to this group:

– two flakes with denticulated-notched retouch on the circumference (Fig. 4:4–5);

– a backed tool on a thick flake with a convex blunted back (Fig. 4:6);

– two transversal truncations in the proximal part of irregular blades (Fig. 4:7–8);

– an oblique truncation on a partially retouched bladelet (Fig. 4:9); and

– a bladelet with denticulated unilateral retouch.

3) The only Paleolithic find is a backed bladelet with transversal retouch (probably a fragment

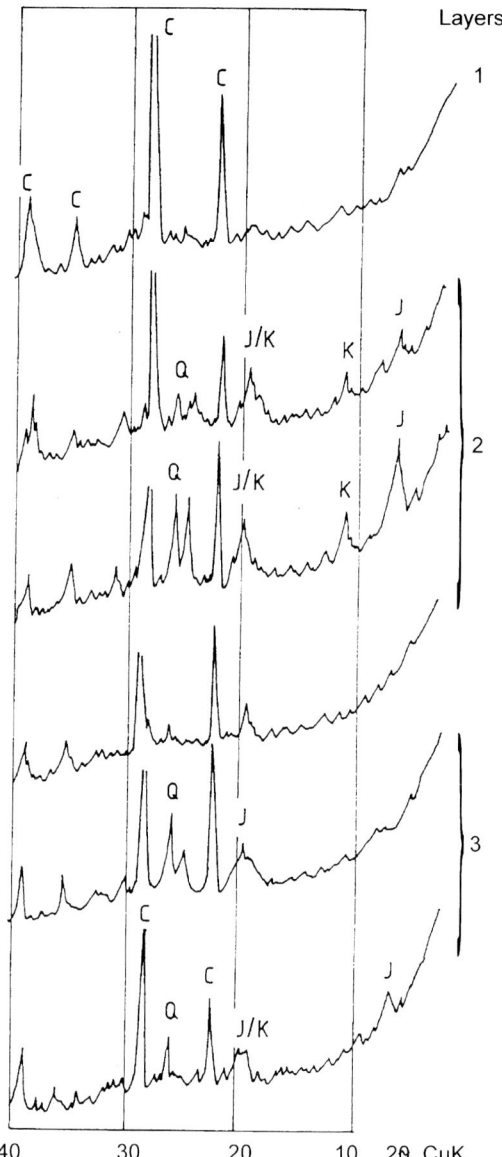

Fig. 3. Klisoura Gorge, Cave 7. X-ray diffraction patterns for samples from layers 1–3

of a rectangle), made from radiolarite (Fig. 4:10).

Seven radiolarite cores were found on the surface, but chronologically could equally be either Mesolithic or Late Paleolithic:

– four short, single-platform cores for flakes and blades with broad, convex flaking surfaces; the platforms are partially prepared by two to four flake scars (Fig. 4:11–14);

– two double-platform cores with a succes-sive change of orientation on the opposite sides of a core. The flaking surfaces are flat, with blade-flake scars (Fig. 4:15,16);

– one multi-platform, residual flake core (Fig. 4:17).

To this group belongs a core tablet detached short, single-platform core made from radiolarite (Fig. 4:18).

Layer 1

Layer 1 yielded 287 lithic artifacts (Table 1). Cores and corresponding debitage allow us to dis-tinguish three reduction systems:

1) a reduction sequence in which the distal part of the radiolarite nodule was removed to shape the platform; subsequent flakes and blade-lets were detached from the convex surface of the core. As the flaking surface was broadened, it was rounded and extended onto the core sides remov-ing cortical surfaces (Fig. 5:1–2) until the flaking surface extended on the whole circumference of the core (Fig. 5:3). These cores were no more than 3.2 cm high, and blanks obtained from them were shorter than 3 cm.

2) a system of shaping the platform by de-taching one large flake and by commencing the reduction from the narrower face of a radiolarite nodule. As the flaking surface became narrower in the distal part, regular bladelets were obtained whose length did not exceed 3–3.2 cm (Fig. 5:4–5). The preparation of some of the cores of this type is similar to the preparation of "wedge cores" (Fig. 5:6–7).

Table 1

Major artifact groups in Cave 7, layer 1

Major group	N	%
Cores	11	3.83
Splintered pieces	7	2.44
Retouched tools	17	5.92
Blades & blade fragments	15	5.22
Flake & flake fragments	35	12.19
Chips	175	60.97
Shatter	27	9.40
TOTAL	**287**	**99.97**

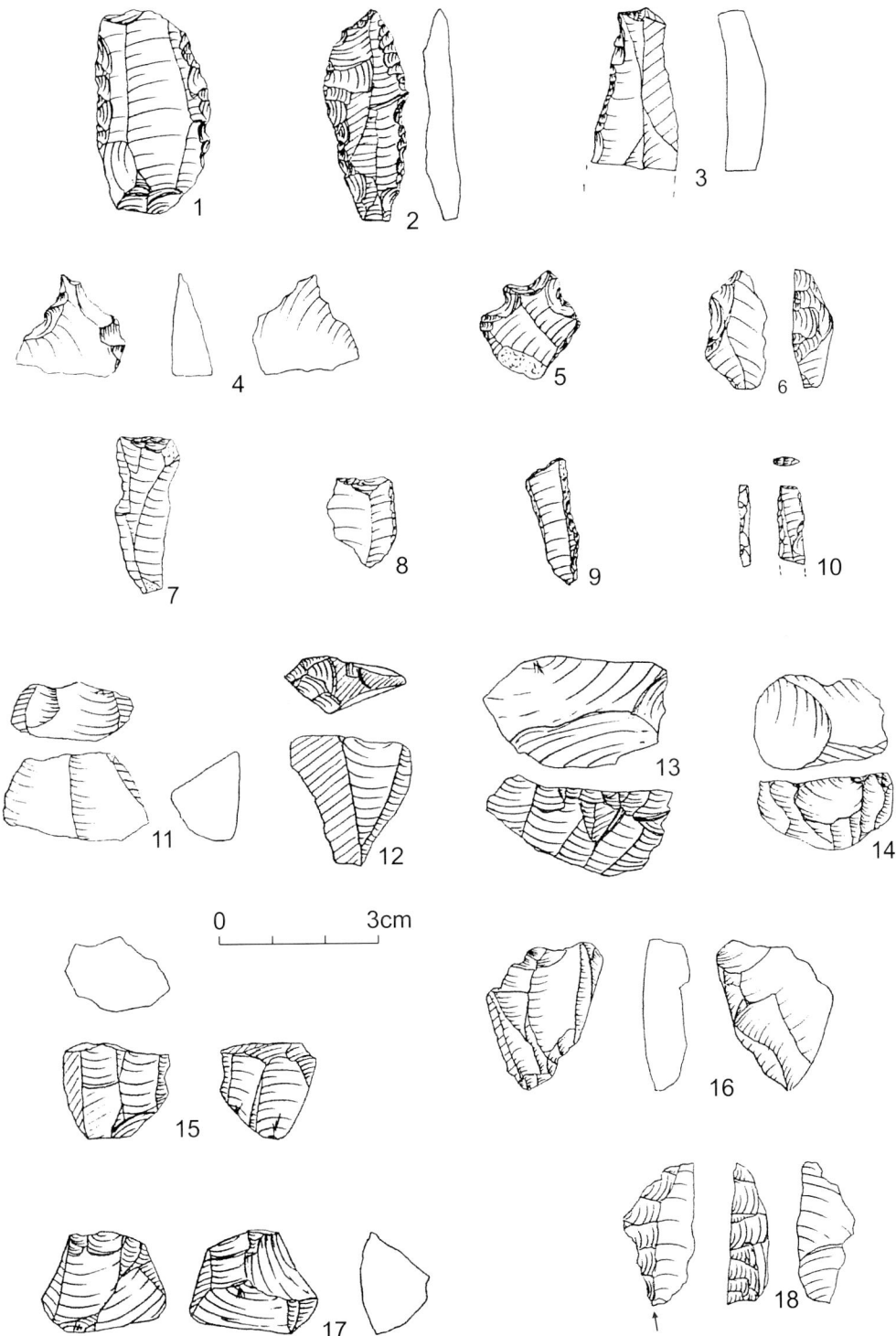

Fig. 4.   Klisoura Gorge, Cave 7. Surface lithic finds (1–18)

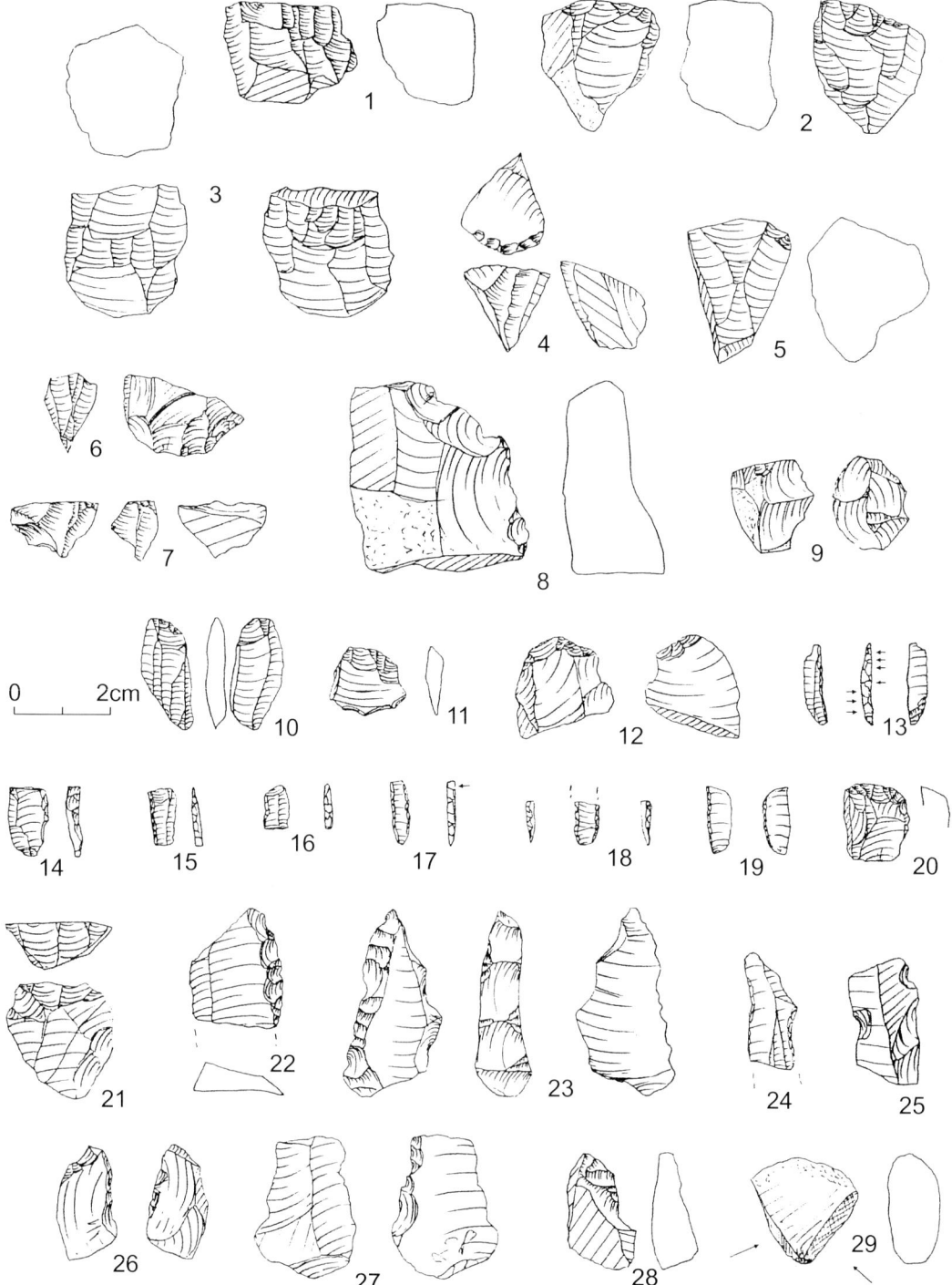

Fig. 5. Klisoura Gorge, Cave 7. Lithic artifacts from layer 1 (1–29)

3) discoidal cores, from which one-sided and two-sided flakes were removed (Fig. 5:9). The latter specimens were distinctly smaller and did not exceed 1–1.5 cm in length.

In addition, the splintered technique was used for the production of microlithic bladelets and flakes. Splinters were made on chunks (Fig. 5:10) or flakes (Fig. 5:11). This technique was also used for thinning the proximal parts of flakes (Fig. 5:12).

Backed bladelets (seven) are represented by the following radiolarite specimens:

– a fine bladelet with a straight blunted back with bipolar retouch, the base is thinned by flat retouch. This specimen matches the definition of a microgravette (Fig. 5:13);

– a proximal fragment of a backed bladelet (Fig. 5:14);

– two mesial fragments of backed bladelets. Both exhibit some kind of impact fracture in the distal part and suggests that they were hafted as arrowpoints (Fig. 5:15–16);

– two proximal fragments of bladelets with steep, bilateral retouch; the butts have been preserved (Fig. 5:17–18); and

– a Dufour type bladelet with fine, alternate retouch (Fig. 5:19).

Two short endscrapers made from radiolarite are: a short microlithic specimen on a flake (Fig. 5:20) and a bigger specimen with a high front, also on a flake (Fig. 5:21).

Two sidescrapers: one is lateral and convex made from banded flint (Fig. 5:22), the other is bi-lateral, shaped by slightly denticulated retouch, with a kind of blunted back formed by denticulated retouch, made from radiolarite (Fig. 5:23).

Five notched-denticulated tools from radiolarite are represented by blade specimens with lateral retouch (Fig. 5:24–25), and by flake, lateral or transversal, specimens (Fig. 5:26–28).

Layer 1 yielded a hematite pebble with traces of abrasion on both sides (Fig. 5:29). A discoidal core made from hematite was also present (Fig. 5:8).

The most important raw material worked on the site was local red radiolarite (Table 2) of which the majority of retouched tools are made. Occasionally greenish radiolarite was used. The next, most important raw material is local brown flint, which occurs predominantly as chips.

Table 2

Raw materials in Cave 7, layer 1

Raw material type	N	%
Brown flint	85	29.62
Black flint	17	5.90
White flint	1	0.35
Beige flint	3	1.05
Quartz	1	0.35
Radiolarite (reddish)	171	59.58
Radiolarite (greenish)	5	1.74
Chalcedony	1	0.35
Jasper	1	0.35
Hematite	2	0.70
TOTAL	**287**	**99.99**

Other raw materials are represented by individual debitage products, specifically, chalcedony, jasper, beige and white flint which are likely extralocal. In any case these raw materials have not been found either in the Klisoura Gorge or in the Prosymna Basin.

Layer 2

Layer 2 contained 234 lithic artifacts (Table 3). Blanks were obtained exclusively from local radiolarites. The production technique for the reduction of low single-platform, blade-flake cores was somewhat similar to that found in layer 1, but flaking surfaces, located on broad, convex surfaces, extended only partially to the sides. No

Table 3

Major artifact groups in Cave 7, layer 2

Major group	N	%
Cores	7	2.99
Splintered pieces	15	6.41
Retouched tools	6	2.56
Bladelets & bladelet fragments	17	7.26
Flakes & flake fragments	56	23.93
Chips	131	55.98
Shatter	2	0.85
TOTAL	**234**	**99.98**

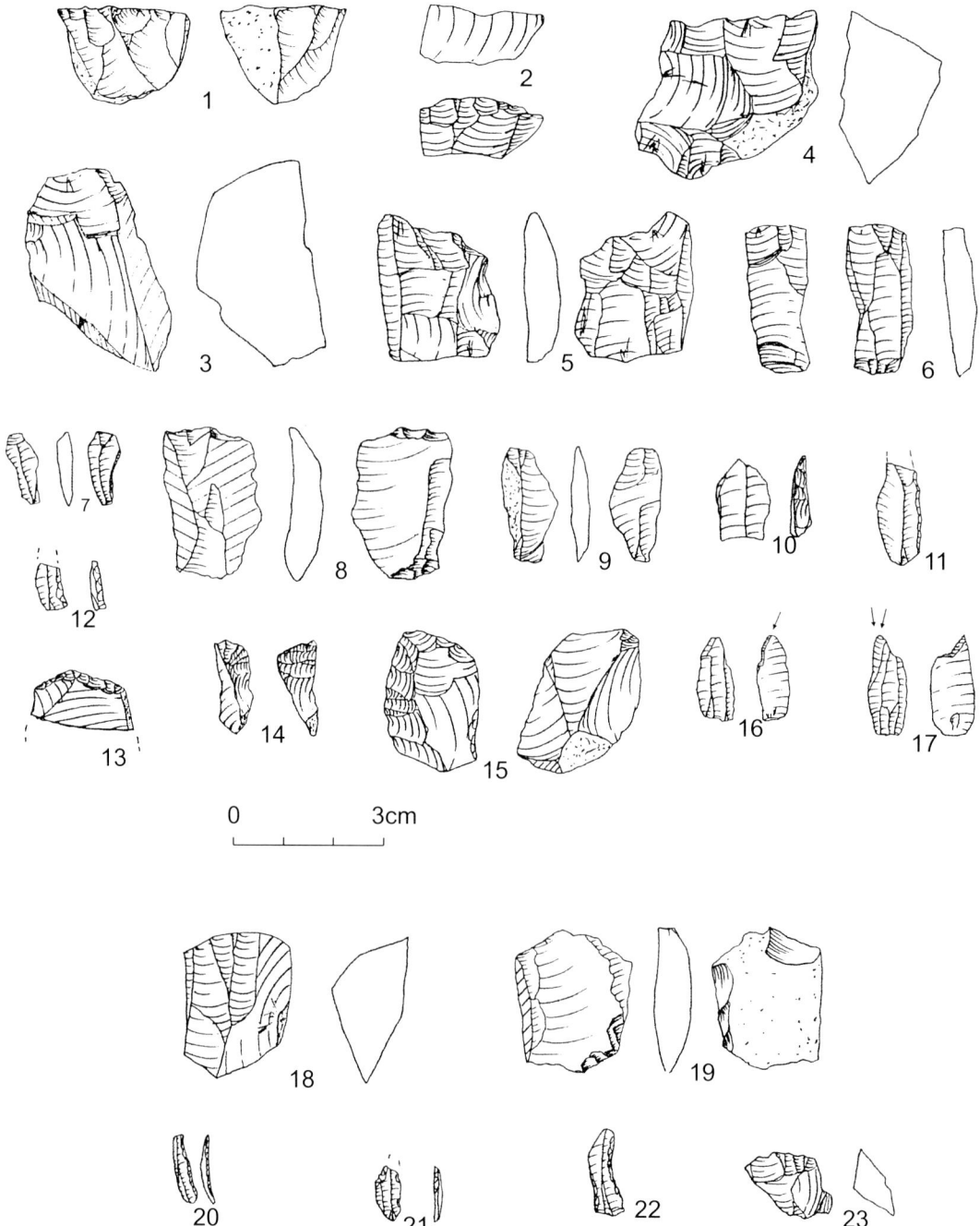

Fig. 6.   Klisoura Gorge, Cave 7. Lithic artifacts from layer 2 (1–22)

Table 4

Raw materials in Cave 7, layer 2

Raw material type	N	%
Brown flint	62	26.50
Black flint	17	7.26
Grey flint	2	0.85
Beige flint	2	0.85
Quartz	2	0.85
Radiolarite (reddish)	142	60.68
Radiolarite (greenish)	4	1.71
Quartzite	1	0.43
Silicified limestone	1	0.43
Translucent black flint with grey dots	1	0.43
TOTAL	**234**	**99.99**

Table 5

Major artifact groups in Cave 7, layer 3

Major group	N	%
Cores	3	1.89
Splintered pieces	1	0.63
Retouched tools	4	2.52
Bladelets & bladelet fragments	10	6.52
Flakes & flake fragments	27	17.07
Chips	110	69.60
Shatter	3	1.89
TOTAL	**158**	**100.12**

cores with flaking surfaces over the whole circumference were found (Fig. 6:1–2).

Another reduction technique (applied not only to radiolarites but also to brown-beige flints) was the perpendicular "change-of-orientation" type on flat flaking surfaces. Sometimes the orientation was not changed successively, but alternately. Cores are also fairly small (3.0–3.5 cm) and were used primarily to obtain flakes that were rectangular in shape (Fig. 6:3–5). This technique differed from the discoidal core technique recorded in layer 1. In layer 2, the splintered technique was predominantly used for the production of bladelets. There were two two-sided bipolar splintered pieces, both measuring ca. 3 cm in length (Fig. 6:6) and hypermicrolithic ones (1.3 cm) also two-sided (Fig. 6:7). Additionally, there were splintered pieces on flakes, which could have been used as chisel tools (Fig. 6:8–9). All of the splintered pieces, except one from brown flint, are made from radiolarite.

Layer 2 yielded only three fragments of backed bladelets made from various raw materials such as gray banded quartzite, good quality gray flint and radiolarite. There were: a specimen with a broken off distal end and fairly fine marginal retouch (Fig. 6:11), a distal (Fig. 6:10) and a proximal (Fig. 6:12) fragment of a small backed bladelet.

Two endscrapers were found, one from radiolarite – a fragment of a flake specimen with an angulated front (Fig. 6:13), and the other from black white-spotted flint – a fragment of a longitudinally split high, carenoidal endscraper (Fig. 6:14).

A radiolarite multiple tool was present. It was made on a residual flake core transformed into a splinter; subsequently flat retouch transformed the tool into a convex sidescraper (Fig. 6:15).

Two radiolarite bladelets display a kind of impact fracture that suggests that they were hafted (without retouching) as arrow points (Fig. 6: 16–17).

Layer 2 reveals that primarily radiolarite and brown flint were worked on the site. These materials occur locally in alluvial sediments in Klisoura Gorge and within the limestones in the Prosymna Basin. However, individual tools were made from non-local raw materials such as beige and gray flints and good quality transparent black flint with gray spots were also documented. The quartzite also belongs to this group of non-local materials (Table 4) that were brought to the site.

Layer 3

Layer 3 yielded 158 lithic artifacts manufactured mainly from radiolarite (Table 5). It is difficult to determine which core reduction technique was used because only one core for bladelets, made on a thick radiolarite flake was present. Its flaking surface is situated on the distal part of the flake and extends onto its ventral side thus

Table 6

Raw materials in Cave 7, layer 3

Raw material type	*N*	%
Brown flint	55	34.81
Black flint	15	9.49
Reddish radiolarite	87	55.06
Greenish radiolarite	1	0.63
TOTAL	**158**	**99.99**

approximating the so-called *pièces de la Bertonne* (Lenoir, 1983) or carenoidal transversal burins (Fig. 6:18).

Splintered technique is represented by only one one-sided splintered piece made on a radiolarite chunk (Fig. 6:19).

All the backed bladelets are hypermicrolithic (1.2–1.6 cm long), made from radiolarite and local flint:

– a simple backed bladelet (Fig. 6:20);
– a bladelet with an oblique blunted back (Fig. 6:21);
– a bladelet with bilateral, concave, obverse retouch, resembling Dufour type bladelets (Fig. 6:22).

A fragment of a short radiolarite endscraper on a flake (Fig. 6:23) was also present.

In layer 3 the ratio of the two, most frequently used raw materials (red radiolarite, brown flint) is similar to that in layer 2 (Table 6).

The radiocarbon date for layer 1 suggests that it was contemporaneous with lithic phase VI in the Franchthi Cave. The morphology of microliths exhibits both similarities and differences between the assemblage from layer 1 and the Franchthi Cave. In both assemblages the microliths are hypermicrolithic and bladelets with a bilateral blunted back are present (cf. Perlès, 1995: Fig. 2:29–33). The dissimilarities are the absence of geometrical forms in Cave 7 layer 1 that are represented in phase VI in the Franchthi Cave by lunates (Perlès, 1995: Fig. 5:24–35) and triangles (Perlès, 1995: Fig. 5:1–23). Moreover, in Cave 7 no traces of microburin technique have been recorded. This technique is well represented in phase VI in the Franchthi Cave (12% of all tools).

The distinct character of the assemblage in Cave 7 layer 1 is further emphasized by the presence of a microgravette (Fig. 5:13)—a type of a microlith that is unknown in the Epigravettian of Franchthi Cave. On the other hand, such a microgravette is a stable element of the Late Epigravettian in the Balkans. For example, in Temnata Cave, microgravettes with flat retouch on the base occur in level I (Sirakov *et al.*, 1994: Pl. 29:8), in level Ia/II (Sirakov *et al.*, 1994: Pl. 20:7.11) and in level III (Sirakov *et al.*, 1994: Pl. 16:3) in the period 13,600 ± 200 to 13,920 ± 480 B.P. In Epirus, such forms are recorded in layer 3 of Kastritsa Cave (Adam, 1989: Pl. 25:9) and dated to ca. 13,400 B.P. In Klithi Cave in Epirus, similar microgravettes are documented in the levels containing the Final Epigravettian accompanied by microburin technique (Adam, 1989: Pl. 36:5, 7). Thus, the microgravettes described above represent an earlier tradition of the Balkan Epigravettian, whereas in Cave 7 layer 1 their character is residual.

The differences between Cave 7 layer 1 and Franchthi Cave phase VI can be partially explained by the small number of artifacts in the assemblage of layer 1. This small quantity of artifacts could explain the lack of geometrical forms. Another explanation is the unique style of microlith production in layer 7, which was not the product of the microburin technique.

Chronologically, Cave 7 layer 2 and layer 3 are probably close to Franchthi Cave phase V, which has been dated to ca. 11,240 ± 140 years B.P. In techno-typological terms, the differences between the microliths in Cave 7 layers 2–3 and in phase V are the same as the dissimilarities revealed in the comparison between layer 1 and phase VI, namely:

– absence of double-backed bladelets in layers 2–3. In phase V of the Franchthi Cave, there are bigger forms of backed bladelets resembling Font Yves points (Perlès, 1995: Fig. 3:11–14);
– absence of geometrical forms represented by microlithic triangles in layers 2–3;
– absence of microburin technique in layers 2–3.

The only element in common could be a microlithic truncation from layer 3 (Fig. 6:21) that resembles hypermicrolithic truncations from Franchthi Cave phase V (Perlès, 1995; Fig. 3:19).

CAVE 4

Basically, Cave 4 is a shallow rockshelter ca. 15 m2 in area (Fig.7). The sediments in the cave are partially disturbed by contemporary anthropic activity. In the shelter, two trenches measuring 1-x-1 m were dug (Fig. 8). Trench B contained only mixed sediments, disturbed when the shelter was used as an animal pen and its floor was leveled. Also in trench A, as far as layer 3, the sediments were disturbed. They contained Late Paleolithic lithic artifacts, bones and ceramics from the Neolithic and the Bronze Age.

Beginning with layer 4, which is a *terra rossa* type clay incorporating small fragments of limestone, Late Paleolithic lithic finds were found *in situ* (Figs. 9–10). Below layer 4 similar clay occurred, but with only a small quantity of limestone fragments. Mineralogical analysis has shown that the two clay layers are built of poorly crystallized calcite mixed with the clay minerals illite and quartz.

Lower down, layer 6 was comprised of brown clay with a large component of weakly weathered fine limestone debris (accounting for 40–50% of the volume of the layer). The bone assemblage from this layer was radiocarbon dated to 11,600 ± 350 (Gd-15520). This clay overlies redeposited material of the *terra rossa* type containing a small quantity of limestone debris (layer 7). Limestone blocks are present only close to the entrance to the rockshelter.

On this basis we can merely suggest that the sequence in Cave 4 represents two warmer and wetter periods in layer 4, layer 5 and layer 7, which were separated by a colder, more humid episode in layer 6. This permits us to attempt to date the entire sequence of layers 4–7 to the Alleröd and Bölling Interstadials with the possible intrusion of the oscillation of Dryas II. On the scale of paleoclimatic changes in the Balkans these layers as a whole would correspond to the complex of the Xanthi Warming (Bottema, 1974; Wijmstra, 1969) with steppe conditions and the domination of *Artemisia*, or the conditions of open oak woodland.

Layers 1–3

The material from layers 1–3 consisted of mixed up Neolithic and Paleolithic lithic artifacts.

Fig. 7.   Klisoura Gorge, Cave 4. View of the entrance of the Cave

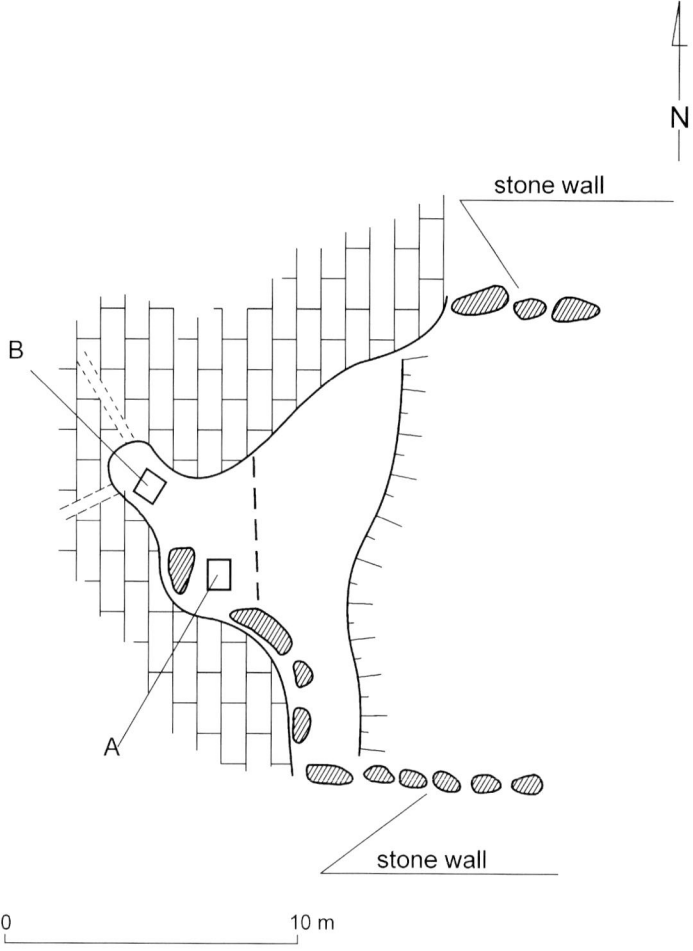

Fig. 8. Klisoura Gorge, Cave 4. Map of the trenches

Among the most characteristic Neolithic artifacts are:

    – a radiolarite blade with alternate retouch (incomplete on one lateral edge) and denticulated, transversal retouch on the break;

    – a kind of raclette on a radiolarite flake (Fig. 11:1);

    – two endscrapers on blades were made from radiolarite can be assigned to the Paleolithic finds (Fig. 11:2–3). However, two fine, bipolar, one-sided splintered pieces from radiolarite are of unknown age (Fig. 11:4–5).

Layer 4: Boundary Zone Between Layers 4–5

    Layer 4 yielded 113 lithic artifacts (Table 7).

Table 7

Major artifact groups in Cave 4, layer 4

Artifact group	N	%
Cores	2	1.76
Splintered pieces	1	0.88
Retouched tools & waste from tool production	8	7.07
Bladelets & bladelet fragments	2	1.76
Flakes & flake fragments	19	16.81
Chips	72	63.71
Shatter	9	7.96
TOTAL	**113**	**99.95**

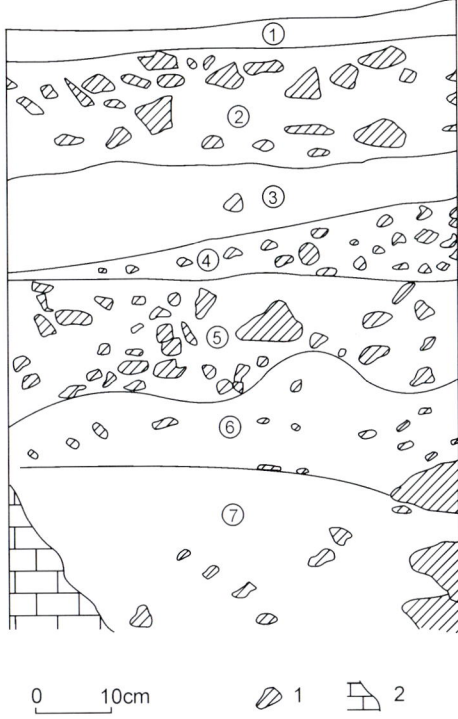

Fig. 9. Klisoura Gorge, Cave 4. Section of the eastern wall of trench A: 1)limestone blocks; 2) bedrock

Fig. 10. Klisoura Gorge, Cave 4. Photo of the eastern wall of the trench (layers 1–5)

The reconstruction of the debitage technique indicates two types of *chaines opératoires*:

a) on radiolarite nodules a core platform was shaped by a transversal scar, subsequently bladelets were detached along the core circumference. Such cores could then be exploited perpendicularly to the original orientation (Fig. 11:6);

b) two-sided discoidal cores were used for the production of small flakes (Fig. 11:7).

Moreover, fine flakes were also obtained from bipolar splintered pieces on radiolarite chunks (Fig. 11:8).

Microliths were produced from bladelets (a backed bladelet with a truncated base, from radiolarite; Fig. 11:9) or on flakes – even cortical ones (a proximal fragment of a backed blade with the tip shaped as *piquant-trièdre*; Fig.11:10).

For the production of microliths, the microburin technique was employed and this is evident by the presence of three microburin – all of the Krukowski type (Fig. 11:11–12) were detached from distal parts of backed pieces; one microburin

was detached from a thin splintered piece (Fig. 11:13).

A hypermicrolithic endscraper with unilateral retouch was made on a partially cortical radiolarite blade (Fig. 11:14).

There were also a retouched bilateral radiolarite bladelet (Fig. 11:15) and a flake with alternate, notched-denticulated retouch in the distal part (Fig. 11:16).

Only local raw materials were used, and red radiolarite is twice as frequent as brown flint (Table 8).

Layer 5

In layer 5, a total of 224 lithic artifacts were recorded. The dominant technique in this layer is the single-platform blade-flake core technique. Usually flat radiolarite fragments were used after the platform had been prepared by one blow, flaking surfaces were installed on two parallel, broader surfaces. As a result there are cores with

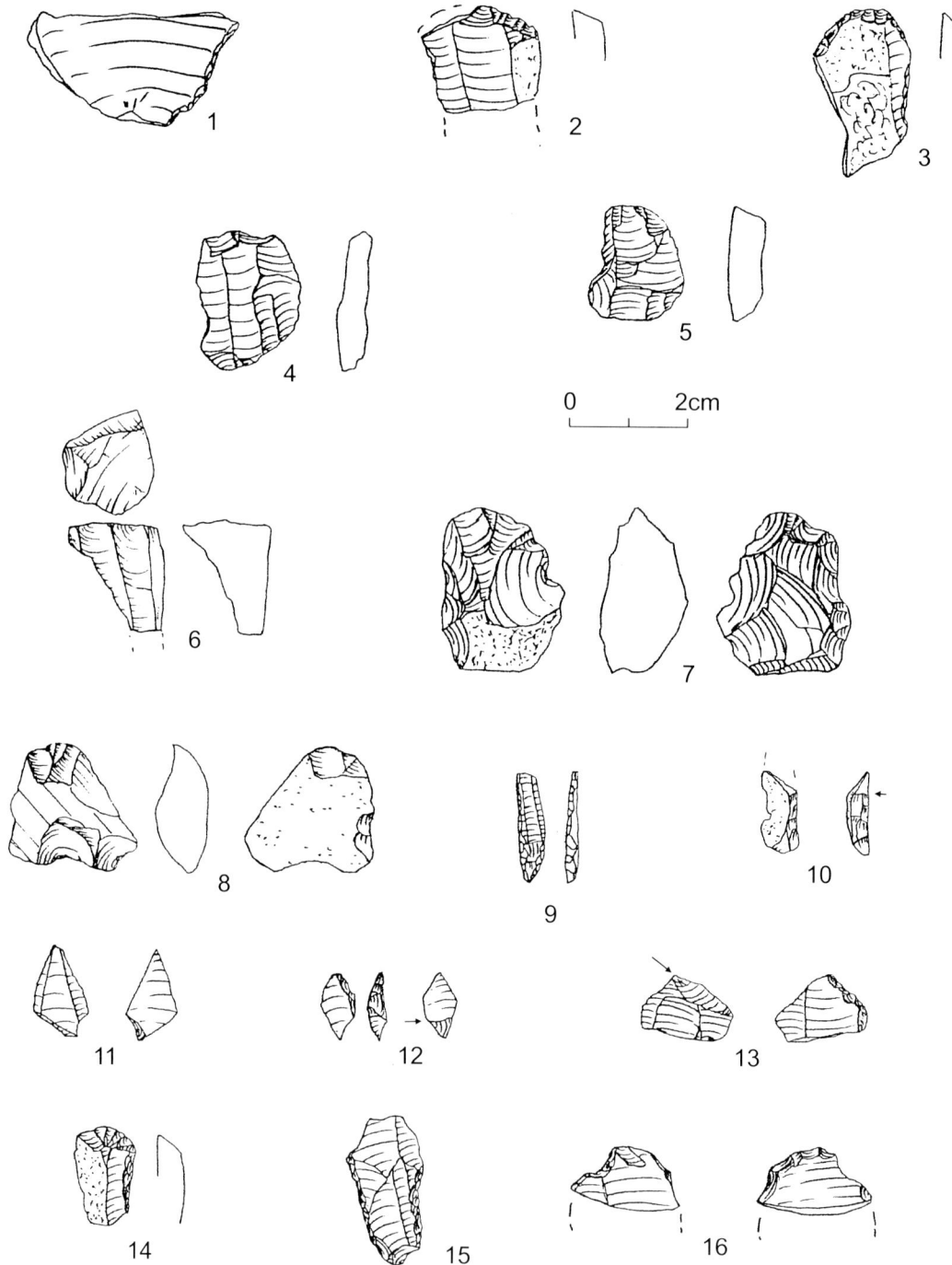

Fig. 11. Klisoura Gorge, Cave 4. Lithic finds from layers 1–3 (1–5) and layer 4 (6–16)

Table 8

Raw materials in Cave 4, layer 4

Raw material type	N	%
Brown flint	36	31.85
Black flint	3	2.65
Reddish radiolarite	74	65.48
TOTAL	**113**	**99.98**

Table 9

Major artifact groups in Cave 4, layer 5

Major artifact group	N	%
Cores	8	3.57
Splintered pieces	4	1.79
Retouched tools	16	7.14
Bladelets & bladelet fragments	21	9.38
Flakes & flake fragments	31	13.84
Chips	106	47.32
Shatter	38	16.96
TOTAL	**224**	**100.00**

Table 10

Raw materials in Cave 4, layer 5

Raw material type	N	%
Quartz	1	0.45
Chalcedony	3	1.33
Brown flint	43	19.19
Black flint	8	3.57
Beige flint	1	0.45
Reddish radiolarite	152	67.83
Greenish radiolarite	11	4.91
Undetermined	5	2.23
TOTAL	**224**	**99.96**

the flaking surface on one or both faces, extending onto the narrow sides of a core (Fig. 12:1–2). These cores exhibit, sometimes, detachments from the opposite core tip that aim not so much at commencing bipolar reduction but rather at the thinning of the distal part of a core which enabled the artisan to obtain blades from the side of the core (Fig. 12:3). One of the cores representing this reduction system has a perpendicular scar that indicates an attempt at a change of the orientation of the debitage (Fig. 12:4).

Attempts can also be seen at starting core reduction on radiolarite nodules from the narrower side, which facilitated the removal of regular blades (Fig. 12:5–6).

In the group of eight microliths there were three fragments of backed bladelets with a straight blunted back shaped by steep, uni- or bipolar retouch. The bases of the two specimens (Fig. 12:7–8) and one mesial part (Fig. 12:9) have been preserved.

The distal part of a backed piece was shaped as *piquant-trièdre* (Fig. 12:10). Three microliths have a convex blunted back. Of these two are hypermicrolithic resembling lunates (Fig.12:11–12), and one is a fragment of the proximal part (Fig.12:13). Only one backed piece has an angulated back with a form closer to a scalene triangle (Fig. 12:14).

One specimen with an arched blunted back was made from transparent chalcedony, but the remainder of the backed blades were made from local radiolarite. Two microburins (one brown flint; one radiolarite) removed the distal part of bladelets with retouched lateral sides (Fig. 12:15) or lateral notches (Fig. 12:16).

Two endscrapers from radiolarite and black flint are: a very short, blade specimen (Fig. 12:17) and the edge or the front of a high carenoidal endscraper (Fig. 12:18).

Two notched tools are made on radiolarite flakes (Fig. 12:19–20) and one such tool is made on a brown flint flake (Fig. 12:21). Moreover, a lateral sidescraper made on a radiolarite splintered piece (Fig. 12:22) was present.

Splintered technique could have been used both to produce blade and flake blanks (Fig. 12:23) and for the thinning of flakes that themselves came from splintered pieces (Fig. 12:24).

Layer 6

A total of 242 lithic artifacts have been recorded (Table 11). Local processing of radiolarites was carried out and represented in the sequences of reduction of small cores for bladelets and for flakes:

– the first sequence is based on the preparation of the platform by a transversal blow and by

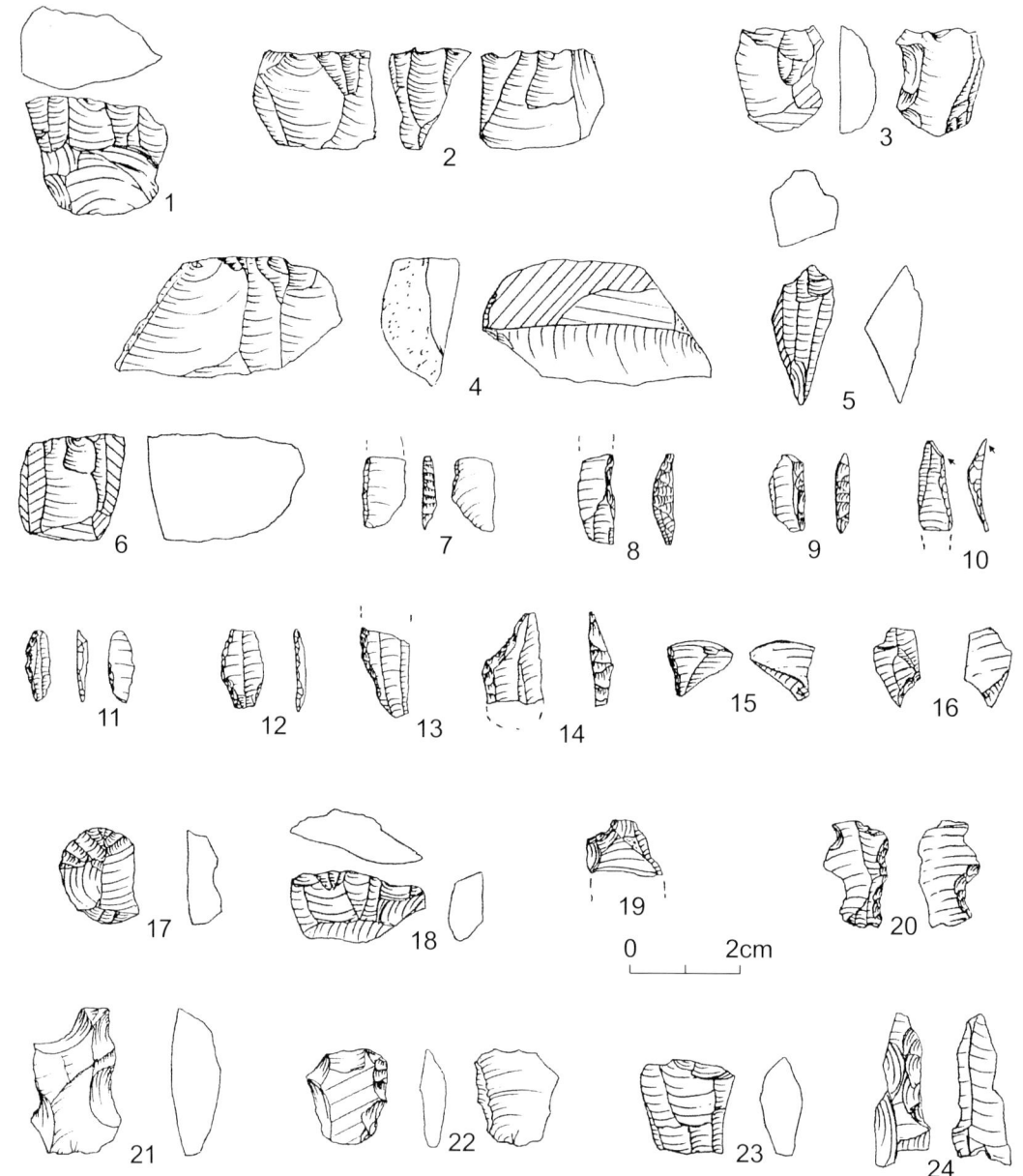

Fig. 12. Klisoura Gorge, Cave 4. Lithic finds from layer 5 (1–24)

detaching bladelets from this platform on the convex flaking surface. As the flaking surface became flatter also flakes were detached. The length of these flakes did not exceed 2.5 cm (Fig. 13:1–2),

– a different reduction sequence is documented by two symmetrically located platforms prepared by removals inclined towards the back of a core (Fig. 13:3). From such platforms first bladelets and then short flakes – also not exceeding 1.0–1.2 cm – were detached on a common flaking surface.

Splintered technique was more often used for the thinning of flakes or to obtain chisel-like tools

Table 11

Major artifact groups in Cave 4, layer 6

Major artifact group	N	%
Cores	9	3.71
Splintered pieces	6	2.47
Retouched tools	17	7.02
Bladelets & bladelet fragments	21	8.67
Flakes & flake fragments	41	16.94
Chips	124	51.23
Shatter	24	9.91
TOTAL	**242**	**99.95**

Table 12

Raw materials in Cave 4, layer 6

Raw material type	N	%
Quartz	3	1.23
Brown flint	66	27.27
Black flint	10	4.13
White flint	3	1.23
Brown high quality flint with white dots	1	0.41
Reddish radiolarite	136	56.19
Greenish radiolarite	16	6.61
Chalcedony	7	2.89
TOTAL	**242**	**99.96**

(Fig. 13:4) rather than for the production of fine flakes.

Backed pieces in layer 6 (all made from local radiolarite) are represented by two types:

1) backed pieces with a convex blunted back. In this group, three specimens are simple backed pieces (Fig. 13:5–7) and one has a tip shaped as *piquant-trièdre* in a similar way as La Mouillah type points (Fig. 13:8; Tixier, 1963);

– backed pieces with a straight blunted back, including one hypermicrolithic specimen (Fig. 13:9) and one proximal fragment (Fig. 13:10). A small bladelet with fine, partial marginal retouch of the type seen on Dufour bladelets (Fig. 13:11), made from black flint, was also present.

A concave truncation (Fig. 13:12) made from radiolarite can also be assigned to the microlith group.

A Krukowski microburin from brown flint (Fig. 13:13) was shaped by means of microburin technique in the distal part of a backed piece.

Three flakes have partial denticulated-notched retouch (Fig. 13:14–16). They are made from radiolarite and gray flint. A fragment of a flint flake shows lateral denticulated retouch (Fig. 13:17), and a radiolarite splintered piece has a kind of lateral Clactonian notch on the side (Fig. 13:18).

A biconcave sidescraper alternately retouched was made on a radiolarite splinter (Fig. 13:19), and a double lateral simple sidescraper was made on a flake from high quality brown flint (Fig. 13:20).

In the group of sidescrapers belongs a mesial fragment of a lateral convex sidescraper. It exhibits transversal burin blows on the break similar to burin blows on the Corbiac type burins (Fig. 13:21; Bordes 1970).

The majority of artifacts are made from reddish radiolarite; they are twice as numerous as the artifacts made from brown flint (Table 12). The excellent quality brown flint with white spots of which one tool was made and white flint represented among chips can be treated as extralocal raw material.

Layer 7

Layer 7 yielded 148 lithic artifacts (Table 13). Local processing of radiolarites is documented by the debitage and cores which show that flakes were detached from low, single-platform

Table 13

Major artifact groups in Cave 4, layer 7

Major artifact group	N	%
Cores	8	5.40
Splintered pieces	9	6.08
Retouched tools	13	8.78
Blades & bladelet fragments	3	2.02
Flakes & flake fragments	30	20.27
Chips	68	45.94
Shatter	17	11.48
TOTAL	**148**	**99.97**

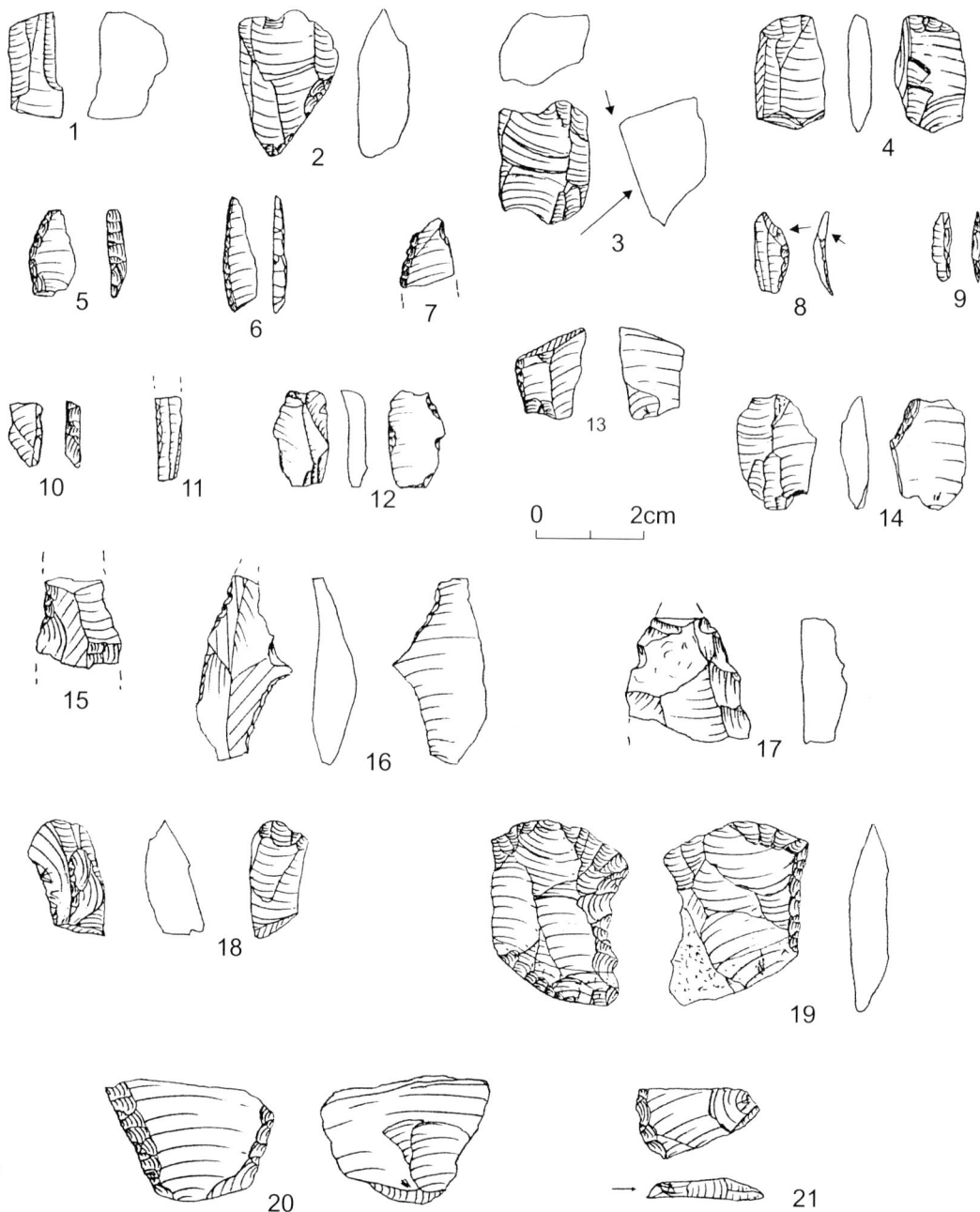

Fig. 13. Klisoura Gorge, Cave 4. Lithic finds from layer 6 (1–21)

cores with a single-blow platform and the flaking surface located on the broader face of a raw material nodule (Fig. 14:1–5). An attempt was made at re-orientating these cores in the final phase of reduction by detaching flakes from the distal part on the opposite (Fig. 14:6) or the same side of a core (Fig. 14:7). Flakes obtained from this group of cores were very short: from 2.0 to 2.5 cm.

There were four backed tools all with a straight blunted back obtained by steep unipolar

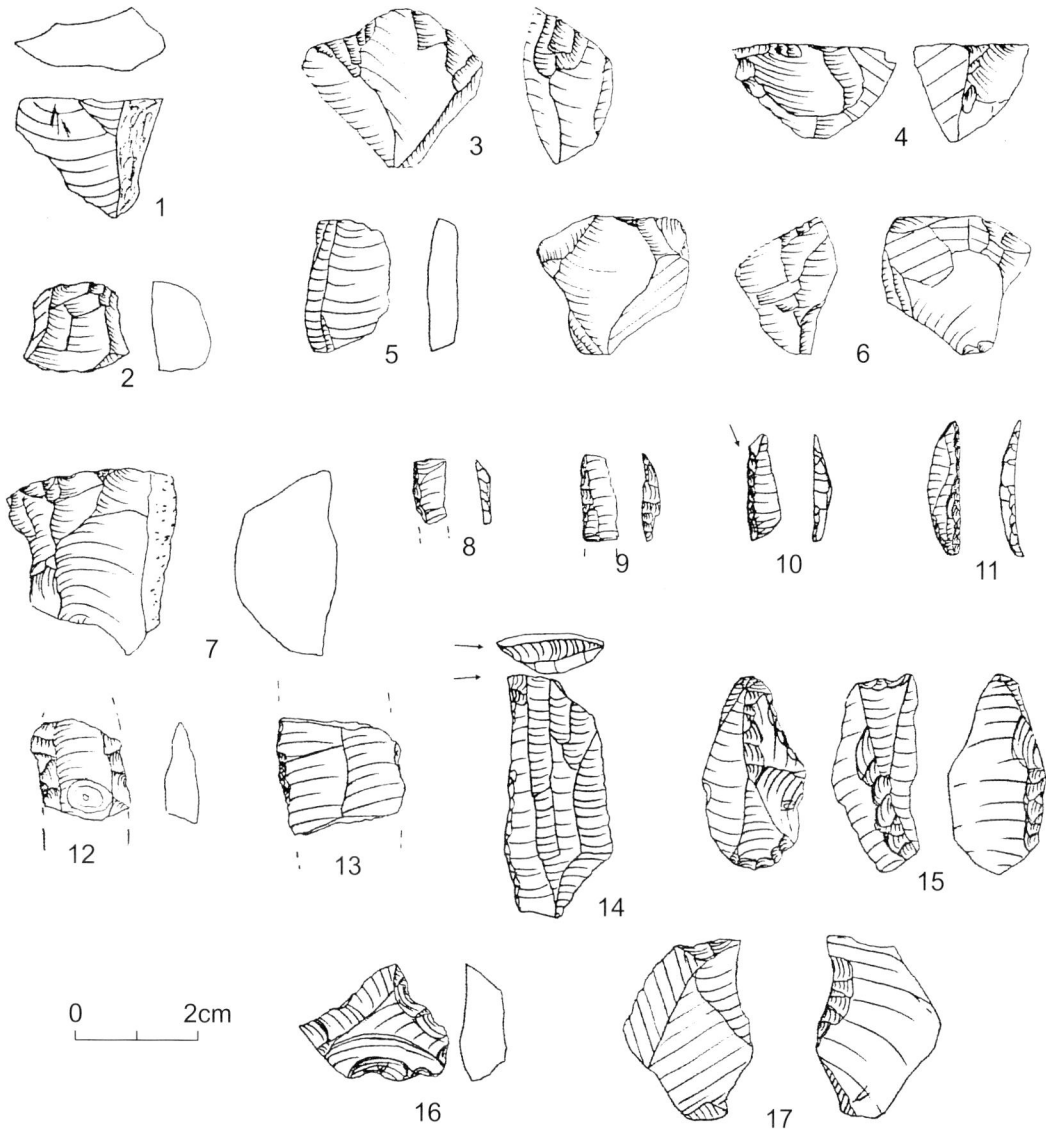

Fig. 14. Klisoura Gorge, Cave 4. Lithic finds from layer 7 (1–17)

retouch. In this group there are two distal fragments (including one with an impact fracture; Fig. 14:8–9), a specimen with the distal part shaped like a *piquant-trièdre* (Fig. 14:10), and a kind of microgravette with partial retouch of the opposite side in the proximal and in the distal part (Fig. 14:11). The latter specimen resembles Pavlov type bladelets which are sometimes described as Pavlov type lunates (Svoboda, 1997: Fig. 3:1–5).

Several bigger blades and blade tools were also recorded in layer 7. Although they were made from local radiolarite they were probably produced away from the site. These are:

– a mesial fragment of a bilaterally retouched blade (Fig. 14:12);

– a mesial fragment of a fairly broad and large blade with partial unilateral retouch (Fig. 14:13);

– a blade with fine discontinuous unilateral retouch and with a kind of Corbiac type burin in the proximal part (Fig. 14:14);

– a robust blade with partial lateral retouch and a burin blow from the retouched notch in the

Table 14

Raw materials in Cave 4, layer 7

Raw material type	N	%
Quartz	1	0.67
Brown flint	24	16.21
Black flint	3	2.02
Reddish radiolarite	99	66.89
Greenish radiolarite	21	14.18
TOTAL	**148**	**99.97**

distal part and partial retouch in the proximal part (Fig. 14:15).

Two notched flake tools, also made from radiolarite, have lateral and proximal retouch (Fig. 14:16–17).

Additionally, a fragment of a denticulated tool, a bladelet with fine partial retouch on one lateral edge and a truncation burin were also found.

Only local raw materials were used in layer 7. Reddish radiolarite distinctly dominates (Table 14). It is possible, however, that some of the artifacts in this layer such as the macroblades were not produced on the site but brought in their final form as blanks.

If we assume that layers 4–7 were deposited during the Xanthi warming (Bölling-Alleröd) then they would be contemporaneous with lithic phases V and IV in the Franchthi Cave (Perlès, 1987). The similarities between the latter two assemblages and Cave 4 are seen first of all in the morphology of microliths and technique of their production:

– in Cave 4 layer 5, backed bladelets with a convex blunted back occur that have counterparts in phase IV from the Franchthi Cave (Perlès, 1995: Fig. 2:30);

– the backed tools in a this layer with an angulated blunted back are similar to the specimens known in phase VI from the Franchthi Cave (Perlès, 1995: Fig. 5:22);

– backed pieces with a convex blunted back from layer 6 (Fig. 12:12–13) have close analogies in phase IV in the Franchthi Cave (Perlès, 1995; Fig. 2:22, 24);

– in all of the layers in Cave 4 microburins, mainly Krukowski type, are present. They were detached from the distal parts of backed bladelets (Fig. 11:11–13, 12:15–16) just like in phases IV and V in the Franchthi Cave (Perlès, 1995; Fig. 2:9–14 and 3:1–3).

An evolutionary tendency that can be traced both in Cave 4 and in phases IV–V in the Franchthi Cave is the decreasing size of blanks and microliths, which become hypermicrolithic forms characteristic for phase VI in the Franchthi Cave and in assemblages from Cave 7.

EVOLUTION OF THE LATE PALEOLITHIC IN THE ARGOLID

A characteristic feature of all of the Paleolithic sequences in Argolid is that there is no continuation between the Pre-Pleniglacial (pre-LGM) settlement and the Late Glacial occupation. The best-known sequence from the Franchthi Cave (Perlès, 1987) exhibits a hiatus between phase II dated at 22,330 ± 350 (and a slightly later phase III whose age has been estimated by C. Perlès as 20/22 Kyr B.P.) and phase IV dated at as early as 12,540 ± 180 years B.P. Phases II and III typically contain simple backed blades (obtuse and pointed), whereas phase IV – in addition to such backed pieces – shows the occurrence of microburin technique and truncated bladelets. Microburin technique in phase IV was used for the shaping of distal ends of backed bladelets with *piquant-trièdre*, similar to La Mouillah type points.

The sequence in Cave 1 at Klisoura shows a hiatus corresponding to the Pleniglacial maximum (LGM) between layers III and 6a (containing the Uppermost Aurignacian) and layer III with simple backed bladelets – dated between 24 to 22 Kyr B.P. – and layers IIa and IIb containing the Epigravettian dated at 16 to 14 Kyr B.P. (Koumouzelis *et al.*, 2000). The distinctive feature of the Epigravettian in these layers is the presence of double backed points and microgravettes with flat inverse retouch distal and/or proximal. In the sequence of Cave 1 another hiatus occurs between the Epigravettian in layer IIa–IIb and the Early Mesolithic from layer 5a, but these layers have not been dated by radiometry. Layer 6 showed a radiometric date of 9,150 ± 220 (Koumouzelis *et al.*, 2000) and based on carbonates.

In central and western Greece, the Early Phase of the Epigravettian, like the western Balkans, is characterized by the presence of shouldered points. Such points appear in the territory of Slovenia (Ovča Jama, 21,740 ± 450) and Croatia (Šandalja II level C, 19,540 ± 500) even before the Pleniglacial maximum (Kozlowski, 1999). In Kastritsa Cave in Greece shouldered points were recorded in strata 5, 3, and 1. These strata correspond to layers 2–15, which provided boundary dates of 19,900 ± 370 (layer 15) and 13,400 ± 370 (layer 2). Strata 5 contained only one shouldered point; they are most numerous in strata 3, and gradually disappear in strata 1. It can be assumed, therefore, that shouldered points appear at Kastritsa as early as the Pleniglacial maximum, whereas the peak of their occurrence falls at the post-maximum period between 18 and 15 Kyr B.P. This type of points could, nevertheless, persist until even 14 Kyr B.P.

Following the shouldered point phase, from 16 to 14 Kyr B.P., the middle phase of the Epigravettian is characterized by the presence of microgravettes (often with flat, inverse retouch) and double backed points. This phase is first known from Cave 1 layers IIa–IIb from Klisoura, but also from the territory of Epirus from the younger portion of the sequence in the Asprochaliko Cave (Adam, 1989).

In Greece, the late phase of the Epigravettian contains predominantly backed bladelets that are commonly accompanied by microburin technique. This trend can be seen at the Peloponnese sites (e.g., Franchthi Cave phases IV–VI) as well as at the sites in Epirus, notably at Klithi (Roubet, 1998), Boila layer IIIb (Kotjabopoulou et al., 1999) and Megalakkos (unit 6). At some sites, geometrical microliths also appear (Franchthi phases V–VI and Megalakkos unit 6; cf., Galanidou 2003:107).

However, the chronological and regional boundaries of the Balkan Epigravettian phases are not precisely defined. We can only document a longer or shorter persistence of the various diagnostic forms. For example, in the Ioannina Lake region, shouldered points persisted longer, whereas on the Pindus Mountain sites the microburin technique could have appeared earlier than in the the Peloponnese region.

The materials from Caves 4 and 7 described in this paper are well within the chronological framework of the Late Glacial and correspond to phases IV–VI in the Franchthi Cave. However, at the same time, the microgravettes are a distinct feature of the Epigravettian tradition of the southern Balkans. Some differences occur in comparison with the central and northwestern Balkans where, besides the general tendency towards hypermicrolithization and geometrization of microliths in the Final Glacial, specific phenomena such as laminarity of backed points and other backed pieces appear (c.f., Mihajlović, 1999: 386). Unlike in Greece, the microburin technique does not occur in these territories, while the splintered technique is commonly used.

In the Late Epigravettian in the Balkans, the on site production of tools from local raw materials is observed. Thus, lower quality materials were used and the number of blanks or tools brought to the site as completed products diminished. This tendency is documented in the sequences in Caves 4 and 7. We can assume that this was the effect of reduced population mobility and greater stability of the settlement (Mihajlovic, 1999). In the northern Balkans open to the Danube basin, this phenomenon is less apparent, although in the Temnata Cave sequence in the Epigravettian layers dated to 13–14 Kyr B.P. the proportion of local raw materials increased – from 43–49% in level III to 67% in level I (Sirakov et al., 1994).

END OF THE PLEISTOCENE AND THE UPPER PALEOLITHIC/MESO-LITHIC BOUNDARY

In the sequences of the Argolid, a chronological and cultural hiatus is evident between the end of the Paleolithic and the Mesolithic. In the Franchthi Cave, the duration of this hiatus is estimated to have been 600–650 years (Farrand, 2003). It is marked at the boundary of lithostratigraphic layers such as in Layer V (a rocky layer with little matrix), by the increased porosity of limestone debris and the distinct roundness of rock fragments. In Layer X1, it shows a considerable degree of chemical corrosion of clastic material with the simultaneous low sedimentation rate. This indicates that Dryas III was probably weakly expressed and may correspond to the hiatus between phase VI dated to 10,800–10,400 years and phase VII of between 9,430 to 9,060 years B.P.

The observation of palynological sequences in Greece (Bottema, 2003) revealed the domination of a steppe environment with a low arboreal component on some sites (10–20%) throughout the period from 13,000 to 9,800 years B.P. (Gramousti, Ioannina I, Xinias). For other sites, open woodland oak with steppe herbs in the period from ca. 13,000 to ca. 11,000–10,500 years B.P., and subsequently the revival of steppe environment with the domination of *Artemisia* (Edessa, Tenaghi Philippon see: Wijmstra 1969). At the beginning of the Holocene, open oak woodland occurs in all of the sequences and only ca. 8,000 years B.P. was this environment replaced by diverse forest with many taxa such as hazel, lime, and elm.

These data can be interpreted as support for the hypothesis that Dryas III was not unequivocally expressed by changes in vegetation in the various environments. We may also explain these data as the result of discontinuity in the paleoclimatic record.

It should be emphasized that in Anatolia, the record of Dryas III was not unequivocal in palynological sequences (Fontugne *et al.*, 1999). At the end of the Pleistocene in Anatolia, two wetter phases occurred when shallow freshwater or brackish lakes, and vegetated marshes appeared in the present-day lake basins. These two wet phases were separated by a brief dry episode. The period of Dryas III is probably seen as such a dry episode without sedimentation. In the relatively numerous profiles in central Anatolia the hiatus corresponding to Dryas III is reflected by the lack of radiometric determinations between 11,000 and 10,000 years ago (Fontugue *et al.*, 1999).

When we interpret the boundary between the Final Paleolithic and the Mesolithic we should draw attention (besides the hiatus mentioned above) to a conspicuous increase in human activity in the Early Mesolithic. This can be seen in the sequences of both Franchthi Cave and in Cave 1 in the Klisoura Gorge where the increased proportion of apatite, which serves as the index for anthropogenic activities is marked in the Mesolithic layer 6 (Koumouzelis *et al.*, 2000).

Unfortunately, because the explored areas in Caves 4 and 7 were small, we could not evaluate the extent of anthropogenic contributions in these caves. We can only estimate that it was smaller in Cave 4 layers 7 and 4 and greater in Cave 7 layers 1–2 and Cave 4 layers 5–6. However, it is difficult to determine the relation between the sedimentation rate and the amount of human activities due to the lack of radiometric dates. It is important to add that in neither Cave 4 or Cave 7 were Holocene sediments recorded. In Cave 4 this could have been the result of shepherds leveling the ground in order to use the place as a shelter for herds. In Cave 7, the absence of sediments was caused by erosion that reached the layer cemented by the dripstone at the Pleistocene/Holocene boundary.

At the Paleolithic/Mesolithic boundary in the Argolid, cultural and economic changes occurred but continuity was also documented. For this reason we cannot unequivocally ascertain whether we are dealing with the same human groups. In the various aspects of culture and economy both continuation and discontinuity are expressed in a variety of ways.

Discontinuity is observed in the economy where the post-glacial adaptation meant that hunting lost its dominant role and other spheres of economy gained importance. This phenomenon in the Argolid is in contrast to northwestern Europe where hunting techniques changed to more individual hunting and trapping methods, but the role of hunting in the Early Mesolithic remained considerable.

It is noteworthy that in the Balkans the role of hunting began to diminish as early as the end of the Pleistocene. In Franchthi Cave the importance of large mammals—bovids and horses—decreased in Phase V (Perlès, 1995:183), and in Phase VI big game remains are scarce representing *Capridae*, *Cervidae* and suids. In these two phases, land snails, notably *Helix figulina*, collected on a mass scale, became important.

Caves 4 and 7 yielded very few faunal remains due to the small area of the trenches as well as the preservation conditions of the strongly fragmented bones. Most of the mammal bones that were discovered are mostly so tiny that the species could not be determined. The few bones that could be identified belong to fallow deer (*Dama dama*). In Cave 4 we collected shells of land snails belonging to genus *Helix* sp. and *Cepaea* sp. This could point to a similar tendency as recorded in phase VI in Franchthi Cave.

Further evidence in favor of discontinuity are burials that appear in the Mesolithic (Cullen, 1995; Kyparissi-Apostolika, 2003) and personal adornments (*Dentalium* sp. beads and pierced pebbles; Perlès 2003), which are unknown in the latest Paleolithic of this area.

Evidence in support of continuity is provided by flake and blade-flake techniques, which were the dominant methods in the Late Paleolithic sites (Caves 4 and 7 in the Klisoura Gorge; phases IV–VI in the Franchthi Cave, among others) and in the Mesolithic layers (Cave 1 at Klisoura, 1 layers 3, 5–5a, 6; Koumouzelis *et al.*, 2003; phases VII–VIII at Franchthi; Perlès 1987). In terms of methods of core exploitation the following reduction sequences can be distinguished in the two periods:

1) single platform cores without preparation of the flaking surface (but, frequently, with a prepared platform) for bladelets and flakes (both detached in all reduction stages) on chunks, pebbles and – possibly – on indeterminate blanks;

2) these cores undergo a change-of-orientation both: orthogonal and opposed; and

3) the same cores, in the final stage of reduction, could be transformed into discoidal cores for flakes, although cores occur that from the beginning had undergone centripetal reduction.

Continuity is, moreover, exhibited by the basic tool kit, mainly by flake tools such as endscrapers and denticulated-notched tools. Comparison of tool morphology shows continuity (e.g., the sequence in the Franchthi Cave). In the final phase before the Mesolithic (phase VI) short endscrapers (Perlès, 1987:Pl. 39:2–9) on flakes are recorded and are similar those flakes from the Early Mesolithic phase VII (Perlès, 1990: Pl.5: 6–7, 9–16). Denticulated tools on flakes (Perlès, 1987:Pl. 38:12–15, 39:11–13 and Perlès, 1990:Pl. 5:13–14, 8:12), and notched tools are alike in the two phases (Perlès, 1987:Pl. 38:16–19 and Perlčs, 1990:Pl. 5:16, 20). Flake forms with lateral retouches are also similar (Perlès, 1990:Pl. 5:8–9). At Klisoura, Caves 4 and 7, similar tool types occur namely: endscrapers (Fig. 4:20–21, 5:13, 11:14, 12:17), denticulated-notched tools (Fig. 134–6; 12:19–20) and flakes with simple lateral retouches (Fig. 4:27; 13:20).

We can, therefore, support the views suggested by Perlès (2003:80) that elements of both continuity and discontinuity can be seen between the end of the Paleolithic and the Mesolithic in Greece. Consequently, we are able to construe various models that would account for the chronological hiatus recorded in the sequences of such sites as Franchthi Cave or Klisoura Cave 1. When we take into consideration the elements of continuity we can assume that at the beginning of the Mesolithic settlements shifted to littoral territories, now submerged, and subsequently returned to areas settled during the Late Paleolithic. We can, moreover, conjecture that the registered elements of discontinuity in the cultural-economic sphere are the effect of environmental changes at the Pleistocene/Holocene boundary. The least plausible hypothesis is the alleged appearance of new population groups in view of the fact the whole of the Mesolithic in the Aegean basin is well rooted in the Epigravettian tradition.

Acknowledgments

Field work in Caves 4 and 7 was supported by the Ephorate for Caves and Palaeoanthropology in Athens, Greece and by Jagiellonian University in Krakow, Poland. The study of materials from Caves 4 and 7 was accomplished with the financial assistance of the Polish Ministry of Science and Informatization, Grant No. 2H01H03924

REFERENCES

ADAM E. 1989. *A Technological and Typological Analysis of Upper Palaeolithic Stone Industries of Epirus, Northwestern Greece*. BAR International Series 512, Oxford.

BORDES F. 1970. Observation Typologiques et Techniques sur le Périgordien Supérieur de Corbiac (Dordogne). *Bulletin de la Société Préhistorique Française*, 67, 4, 105.

BOTTEMA S. 1974. *Late Quaternary Vegetation in Northwestern Greece*. Groningen.

BOTTEMA S. 1994. The prehistoric environments of Greece: a review of palynological record. In: P. N. Kardulias (ed.) *Beyond the site-regional studies in the Aegean Area*, London, 45–49.

CULLEN T. C. 1995. Mesolithic mortuary ritual at Franchthi Cave, Greece. *Antiquity*, 69, 270–289.

FARRAND W. R. 2003. Depositional environments and site formation during the Mesolithic occupations of Franchthi Cave, Peloponnesos, Greece. In: N. Galanidou, C. Perlès (eds.) *The Greek Meso-*

lithic, Problems and Perspectives, British School, Athens, 69–87.

FONTUGNE M., KUZUCUOGLU C., KARABIY-IKOGLU M., HATTE C., PASTRE J. F. 1999. From the Pleniglacial to the Holocene: a chronostra-tigraphy of environmental changes in the Konya Plain, Turkey. *Quaternary Science Review*, 18, 573–591.

GALANIDOU N. 2003. Recessing the Greek Meso-lithic: the pertinence of Markovits Collections. In: N. Galanidou, C. Perlès (eds.) *The Greek Mesolithic Problems and Perspectives*, British School, Athens.

HAHN J. 1984. Südeuropa und Africa. In: *Neue For-schungen zur Altsteinzeit.* München.

KOUMOUZELIS M., KOZLOWSKI J.K., NOWAK M., SOBCZYK K., KACZANOWSKA M., PAWLIKOWSKI M., PAZDUR A. 1996. Prehis-toric settlement in the Klisoura Gorge, Argolid, Greece (excavations 1993, 1994). *Préhistoire Eu-ropéenne*, 8, 143–174.

KOUMOUZELIS M., GINTER B., KOZLOWSKI J. K., PAWLIKOWSKI M., BAR-YOSEF O., AL-BERT R. M., LITYNSKA-ZAJAC M., STWORZE-WICZ E., WOJTAL P., LIPECKI P., TOMEK T., BOCHENSKI Z., PAZDUR A. 2001a. The Early Upper Palaeolithic in Greece: The excavations in Klisoura gorge. *Journal of Archaeological Science*, 28, 515–539.

KOUMOUZELIS M., KOZLOWSKI J. K., ESCUTE-NAIRE C., SITLIVY V., SOBCZYK K., VALLA-DAS H., TISNERAT-LABORDE N., WOJTAL P., GINTER B. 2001b. La fin du Paléolithique moyen et le début du Paléolithique supérieur en Gréce: la séquence de la Grotte no 1 de Klisoura. *L'Anthro-pologie*, 105, 469–304.

KOTJABOPOULOU E., PANAGOPOULOU E., ADAM E. 1999. The Boila rockshelter: further evi-dence of human activity in Voidomatis Gorge. In: G. Bailey, E. Adam, C. Perlès, K. Zachos (eds) *The Pa-laeolithic Archaeology in Greece and Adjacent Ar-eas*, British School, Athens, 19–210.

KOZLOWSKI J. K. 1999. Gravettian/Epigravettian se-quence in the Balkans: environment, technologies, hunting and raw material procurement. In: G. Bai-ley, E.Adam, E. Panagopoulou, C. Perlès, K. Zachos (eds.) *The Palaeolithic Archaeology of Greece and Adjacent areas*, British School, Athens, 319–329.

KYPARISSI APOSTOLIKA N. 2003. The Mesolithic in Theopetra Cave: new data on a debated period of Greek Prehistory. In: N. Galanidou, C. Perlès (eds) *The Greek Mesolithic, problems and perspectives*, British School, Athens, 189–198.

LENOIR M. 1983. La pièce de la Bertonne, fossile di-recteur du Magdalénien ancien? *Bulletin de la Soci-été Préhistorique Française*, 84, 6, 19.

MARKOVITS A. 1928. Apo ta skoti ton spilaion. *Praktika tis Ellenikis Anthropologikis Etaireias*, 45–61.

MIHAJLOVIC D. 1999. Intensification of settlement in the Late Glacial of South-Western Balkans. *Folia Quaternaria*, 70, 385–392.

PERLÈS C. 1987. *Les industries lithiques taillées de Franchthi (Argolide, Grece). Tome I: Présentation générale et industries paléolithiques. Excavations in Franchthi Cave, fascicule 3,*: Indiana University Press, Bloomington, Indianopolis.

PERLÈS C. 1990. Les industries lithiques taillées de Franchthi (Argolide, Grece).Tome II: Les industries du Mésolithique et du Néolithique initial. Excava-tions at Franchthi Cave, 5. Bloomington, Indianopo-lis. Indiana University Press.

PERLÈS C. 1995. La transition Pléistocène/Holocène et le problème du Mésolithique en Grèce. In: V. Villaverde-Bonilla (ed.) *Los ultimos cazadores – Transformaciones Culturales y Economicas Du-rante el Tardiglaciar y el Inicio del Holoceno el Am-biente Mediterraneo*, Alicante, 179–209.

PERLÈS C. 2003. The Mesolithic at Franchthi: an overview of data an problems. In: N. Galanidou, C. Perlès (eds.) *The Greek Mesolithic, Problems and Perspectives*. British School, Athens, 79–88.

REISCH L. 1980. Pleistozän und Urgeschichte des Peloponez. Habilitationschrift. Erlangen (unpub-lished thesis).

ROUBET C. 1998. The backed pieces at Klithi. In: G. Bailey (ed.) *Klithi: Palaeolithic Settlement and Quaternary Landscapes in Northwest Greece, t.1: Excavation and Intra-Site Analysis*, Cambridge, 155–180.

SVOBODA J. 1997. Lithic industries from 1957 area. In: J. Svoboda (ed.) *Pavlov I – Northwest,* Brno. Academy of Sciences of the Czech Republic, 179–210.

TELLENBACH M.1983. Materialien zum Präkera-mische Neolithikum in Süd-Ost Europa. *Bericht der Römisch Germanischen Kommission*, 64, 23–137.

TIXIER P. 1963. *Typologie de L'Epipaléolithique du Maghreb.* Paris.

TURNER C., SANCHEZ GONI M. F. 1997. Late Gla-cial landscapes and vegetation in Epirus. In: G.Bai-ley (ed.) *Klithi in its Local and Regional Setting*, 2, 55–586.

SIRAKOV N., SIRAKOVA S., IVANOVA S., GAT-SOV I., TSONEV T. 1994. The Epigravettian se-quence. In: J. K.Kozlowski, H. Laville, B. Ginter (eds.) *Temnata Cave – Excavations in Karlukovo Karst Area*, 1, 2, 169–314.

WIJMSTRA T. A. 1969. Palynology of the first 30 me-ters of a 130 m deep section in northern Greece. *Acta Botanica Neerlandica*, 18, 4, 511–523

Eurasian Prehistory, 2 (2): 57–73.

SETTLEMENT REORGANIZATION AT THE END OF THE NEOLITHIC IN CENTRAL EUROPE: RECENT RESEARCH IN THE KÖRÖS RIVER VALLEY, SOUTHEASTERN HUNGARY

William A. Parkinson[1], Attila Gyucha[2], Richard W. Yerkes[3], Apostolos Sarris[4], Meredith Hardy[1] and Margaret Morris[3]

[1] *Florida State University, Tallahassee, FL, USA; wparkins@mailer.fsu.edu, merhardy@juno.com*
[2] *Munkácsy Mihály Múzeum, Békéscsaba, Hungary; gyuchaa@freemail.hu*
[3] *Ohio State University, Columbus, OH, USA; yerkes.1@osu.edu, megmorris00@yahoo.com*
[4] *Foundation for Research and Technology–Hellas, Rethymnon, Greece; asaris@ret.forthnet.gr*

Abstract

The transition from the Neolithic to the Copper Age in the eastern Carpathian Basin is characterized by dramatic changes in settlement organization, site distribution, economic practices, and landscape use. Most research into the Early Copper Age Tiszapolgár Culture on the Great Hungarian Plain has focused upon the rich cemeteries that became common during the period. The Körös Regional Archaeological Project's investigations in southeastern Hungary near the modern town of Vésztő have revealed two fortified Early Copper Age settlements nearly identical in size and located less than 100 m apart. Magnetometry, soil chemistry, and excavations at the two sites have revealed a picture of Early Copper Age settlement organization that can be compared to the better known Late Neolithic cultures in the region.

INTRODUCTION: THE TRANSITION TO THE COPPER AGE ON THE GREAT HUNGARIAN PLAIN

The transition from the Neolithic to the Copper Age in central and southeastern Europe coincided with one of the most dramatic transformations in social organization throughout the prehistory of the region. From the southern Balkans to the Austrian Alps, the archaeological record documents significant shifts in metallurgical techniques, the distribution of cultural complexes across the landscape, the organization of settlements, and economic practices (Parkinson *et al.* 2002, 2004; Sherratt, 1983, 1984), all of which suggest a significant restructuring of social and economic relations occurred around 4,500 B.C. (calibrated).

The temporal and spatial scales at which these changes occurred varied throughout the region, even within seemingly homogeneous phy-

siographic units such as the Carpathian Basin. For example, the eastern portion of the Carpathian Basin – the Great Hungarian Plain – underwent rapid, dramatic changes in settlement organization, settlement distribution, and household size. In the western and southern portions of the basin – Transdanubia and northern Serbia – the transition to the Copper Age was much more gradual. It took nearly a thousand years for societies in those regions to acquire the same characteristics (Bánffy, 1994, 1995).

Previous models attributed the changes associated with the end of the Neolithic either to changes in economic organization associated with an increased reliance on domestic cattle husbandry (e.g., Bökönyi, 1988; Bognár-Kutzián, 1972) or to westward migrations onto the plain by Indo-European speaking-groups, who originated somewhere on the south Russian steppes (Gimbutas *et al.* (eds.), 1997).

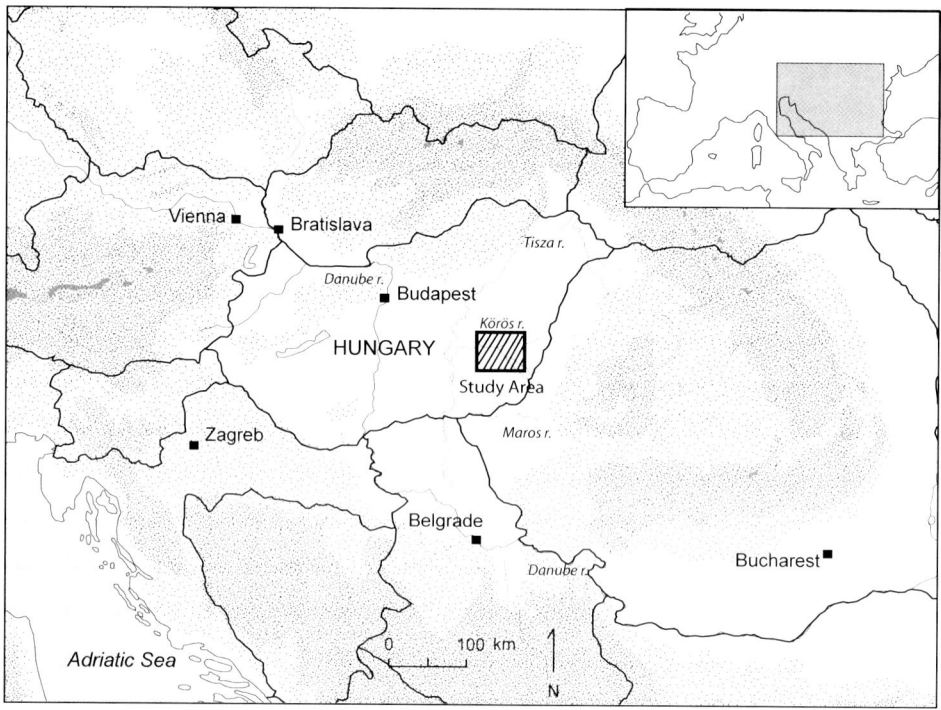

Fig. 1. Map of the Carpathian Basin showing the location of the Körös Regional Archaeological Project study area. Inset shows the location of the Carpathian Basin in Europe. Based on a map initially created by Daniel Sosna, Florida State University

The nature of the more abrupt changes that occurred on the Great Hungarian Plain has been obscured by a lack of systematic research into Early Copper Age settlement organization. While the settlements of the Late Neolithic were the focus of a great deal of systematic exploration throughout the latter half of the twentieth century (e.g., Kalicz and Raczky, 1987; Kalicz and Makkay, 1977), most research into the Early Copper Age focused on the analysis, and re-analysis, of cemetery sites, such as Tiszapolgár-Basatanya (Bognár-Kutzián, 1963; Chapman, 1997; Derevenski, 1997; Meisenheimer, 1989). By the late 1990s only a handful of Tiszapolgár domestic sites had been tested during the course of rescue excavations (Bognár-Kutzian, 1972; Goldman, 1977; Siklódi, 1981, 1982, 1983, 1984).

The Körös Regional Archaeological Project

Since 1998, a collaborative Hungarian-American research project – The Körös Regional Ar-chaeological Project – has been exploring the changes in settlement organization and distribution in the Körös Region of the Great Hungarian Plain associated with the transition to the Copper Age (Fig. 1). Initial research focused on the analysis of settlement patterns associated with the Late Neolithic and the Early Copper Age in northern Békés County (e.g., Parkinson, 1999, 2002). That research built on a long history of settlement archaeology in Hungary (e.g., Ecsedy *et al.*, 1982; Jánkovich *et al.*, 1989, 1998; Sherratt, 1984) and involved surface collections at sites previously identified by Hungarian researchers and comparative stylistic analyses. The settlement distributions led Parkinson (1999, 2002) to argue that the discrete settlement clusters of the Late Neolithic were replaced in the Early Copper Age by more diffuse clusters of settlements that were relocated more frequently across the landscape. In addition, stylistic analyses of ceramic attributes from Early Copper Age settlements throughout the region suggested that the discrete social boundaries that

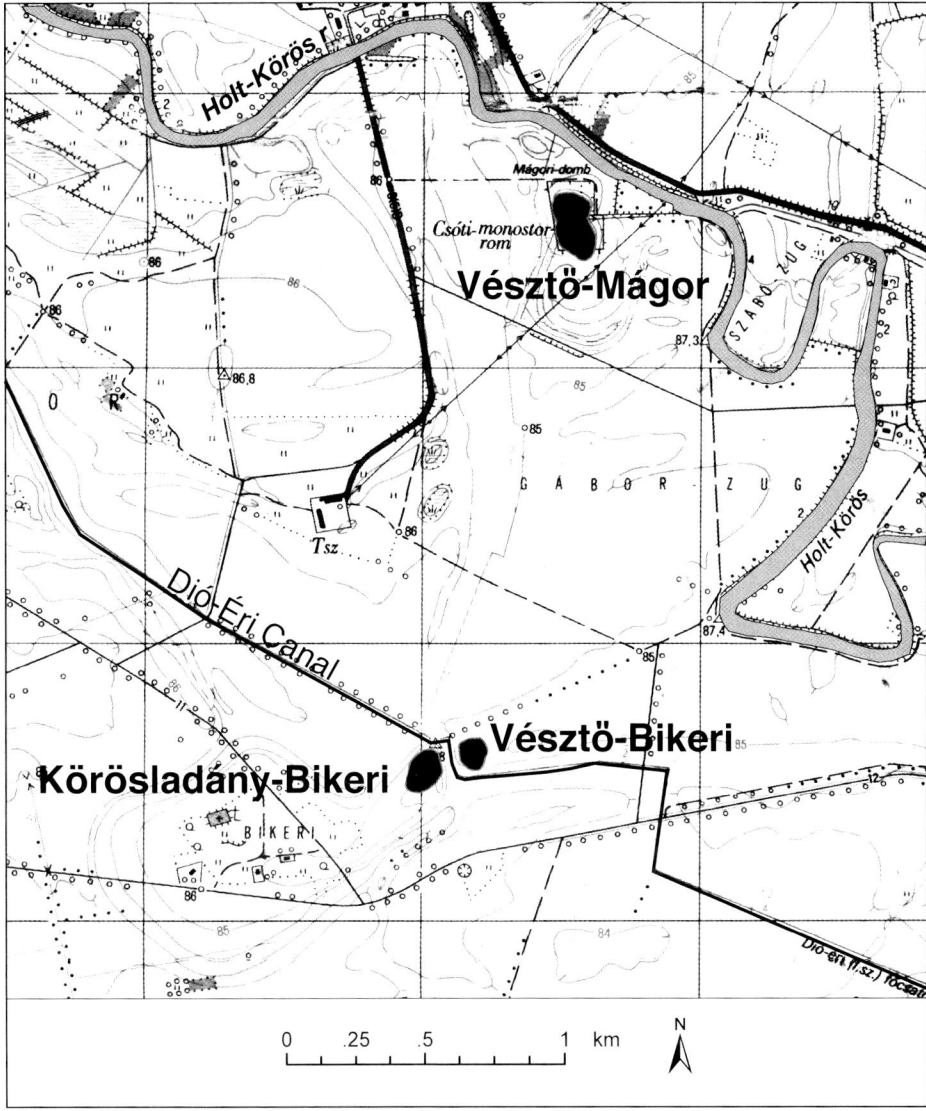

Fig. 2.   Topographic map of Early Copper Age settlements in the Vésztő cluster, showing Vésztő-Mágor (Vésztő 15), Vésztő-Bikeri (Vésztő 20), and Körösladány-Bikeri (Körösladány 14)

had been actively maintained throughout the Late Neolithic became more relaxed and diffuse during the Early Copper Age.

This research helped delineate the relationship between Late Neolithic and Early Copper Age settlement patterns at the regional scale, but in order to provide the kinds of information necessary for clarifying the economic and social changes that occurred at the beginning of the Copper Age it was necessary to investigate one or more Early Copper Age settlements more intensively.

Since 2000, we have been investigating two Early Copper Age settlement sites located approximately 2 km south of the multi-component tell site of Vésztő-Mágor (Hegedűs, 1977, 1982, 1983; Hegedűs and Makkay, 1987; Makkay, 2004). These sites were selected from those revisited in 1998 because of the discrete patterning of archaeological materials on the surface of these

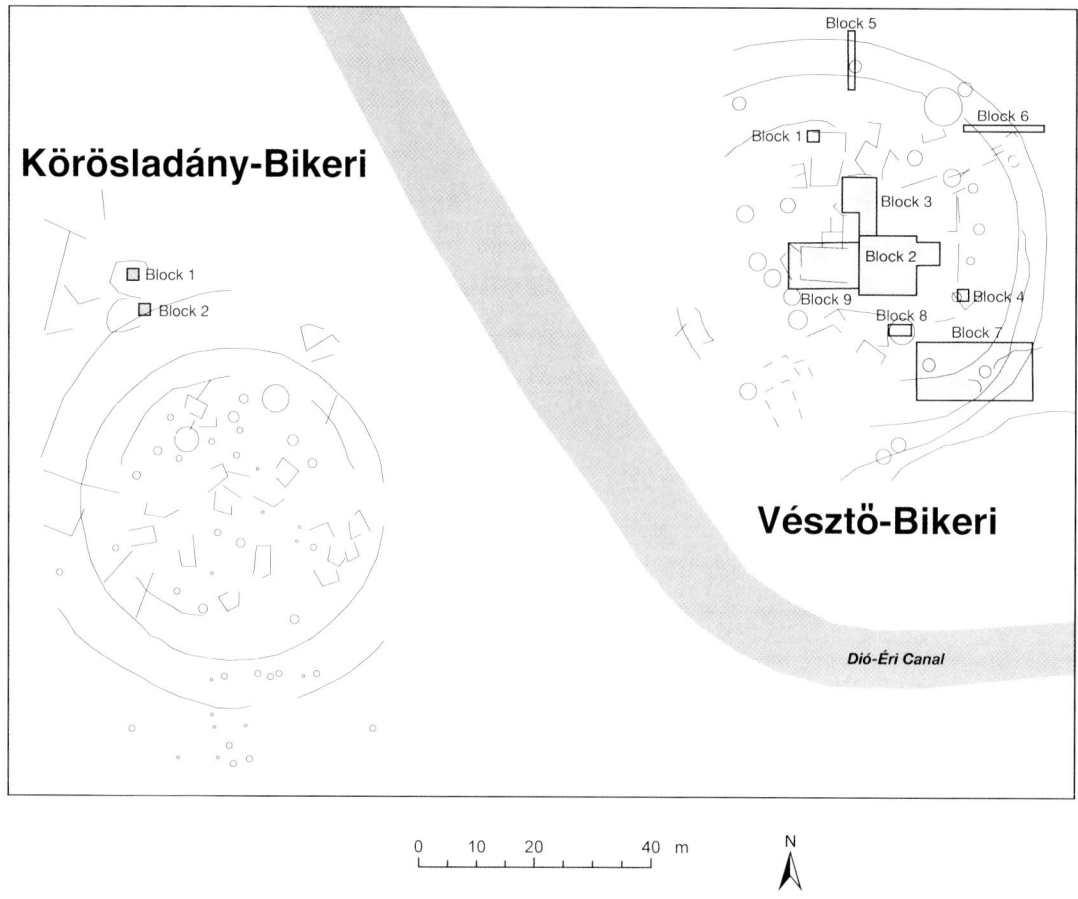

Fig. 3. Map of Vésztő-Bikeri and Körösladány-Bikeri showing location of excavation blocks and magnetic anomalies

adjacent sites, which suggested that their settle-ment features retained a high degree of integrity and were not significantly destroyed by plowing and other post-depositional processes (Fig. 2; Parkinson, 1999: 201, 208–210).

Investigations at Vésztő-Bikeri

A magnetometric survey conducted by Apos-tolos Sarris in 2002 at the site of Vésztő-Bikeri identified several circular anomalies that enclosed a 0.7 ha area containing large rectilinear anoma-lies and other features (Fig. 3; Sarris, 2003; Sarris *et al.*, 2003). These patterns were bolstered by analyses of phosphate levels in soil samples col-lected from the cultural layer across the site. Higher phosphate levels were recorded near the

edges of the site, and lower levels were found to-ward the center of the circular settlement where most of the rectilinear anomalies were located (Fig. 4).

Our excavations established that the circular anomalies surrounding the site were associated with two sets of ditches and an inner series of large post-holes (Fig. 5). The outermost ditch is u-to v-shaped in cross-section and contains at least two fill episodes. The ditch extends ca. 1.6 m be-low the modern surface and is 0.4–1.6 m wide. A shallow, narrow trench (extending 0.8 m below the present surface) lies about 2 m inside the outer ditch. Approximately 3 m inside the middle ditch is a narrower (0.4–0.75 m) wall trench that con-tains several closely-spaced postholes. The large posts in this trench were sunk to a depth 1.7 m

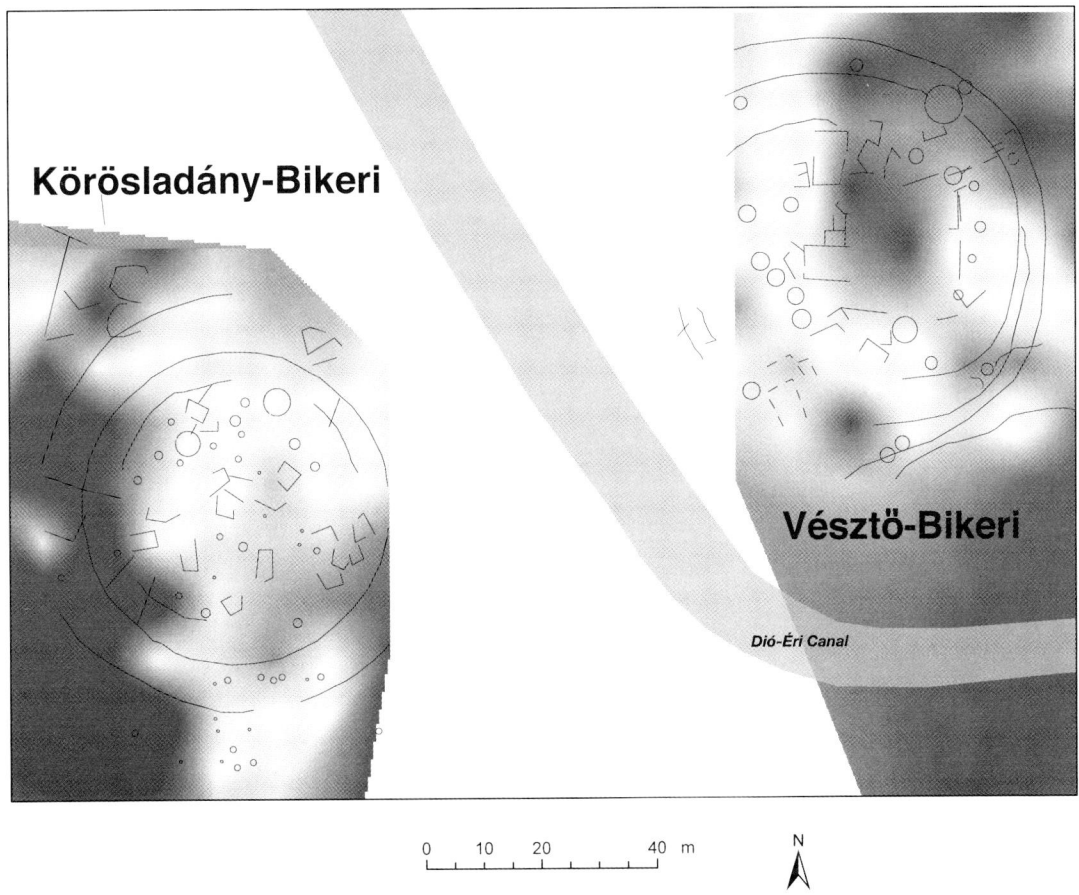

Fig. 4. Map of Vésztő-Bikeri and Körösladány-Bikeri showing location of magnetic anomalies and soil phosphate levels. Higher soil phosphate levels are indicated by lighter colors, lower levels of phosphate by darker levels

below the modern surface. It is believed that the inner ditch contained a wattle-and-daub wall that surrounded the settlement. Approximately 0.6–0.8 m inside the inner wall trench is a series of large post-holes, spaced about 3 m apart. The function of these large postholes (which were sunk about 1 m below the modern surface) remains unclear, but they may have supported a platform built into the inner wall that surrounded the settlement, or have been associated with an internal structure that abutted against the wall (Parkinson *et al.*, 2004; Gyucha *et al.*, in press).

Our excavations at the center of the settlement revealed the remains of three structures, two of which are longhouses oriented east–west that share a common wall foundation trench (Fig. 6). The western structure (Feature 15) measures ca.

14-x-6 m and was built with packed-clay walls set in trenches, while the eastern structure (Feature 4/14) was built with wattle-and-daub walls, also set in trenches. The western structure (Feature 15) was not burned, and seems to have been dismantled and abandoned before the eastern structure (Feature 4/14) was constructed. In fact, a new line of posts were set in the eastern wall trench of Feature 15, and the western wall of Feature 4/14 was built in what was the eastern wall of the western structure. The size of the eastern structure is at least 10-x-6 m, but we were unable to locate the eastern wall trench of the feature. The majority of cultural materials associated with the western feature were recovered from a fill deposit on top of the floor of the feature (Fig. 7), and therefore cannot be associated with the floor itself. By contrast,

Fig. 5.   Photograph of ditches and postholes in Block 7 at Vésztő-Bikeri. Looking northeast. Scale in photo shows 20 cm units. Excavation Block is 10-x-20 m. Photograph by W. A. Parkinson

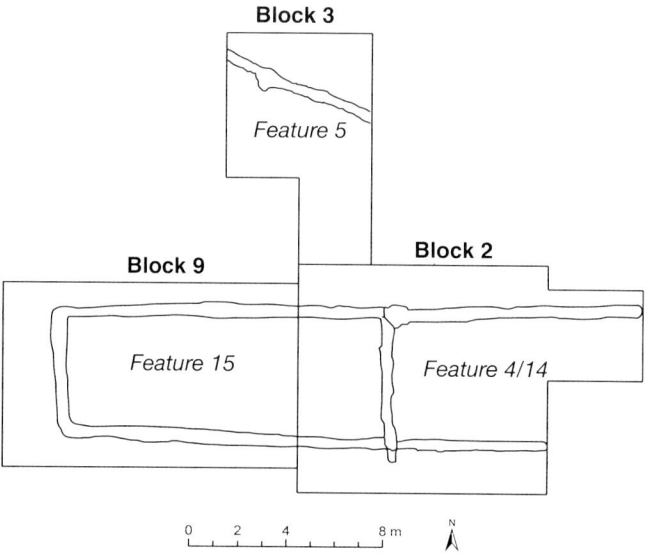

Fig. 6.   Plan map of Blocks 2, 3, and 9, at Vésztő-Bikeri showing the location of wall trenches associated with structures at the center of the site. Based on a map initially created by Drawings by Dóri Kékegyi, Munkácsy Mihály Múzeum, Békéscsaba, Hungary

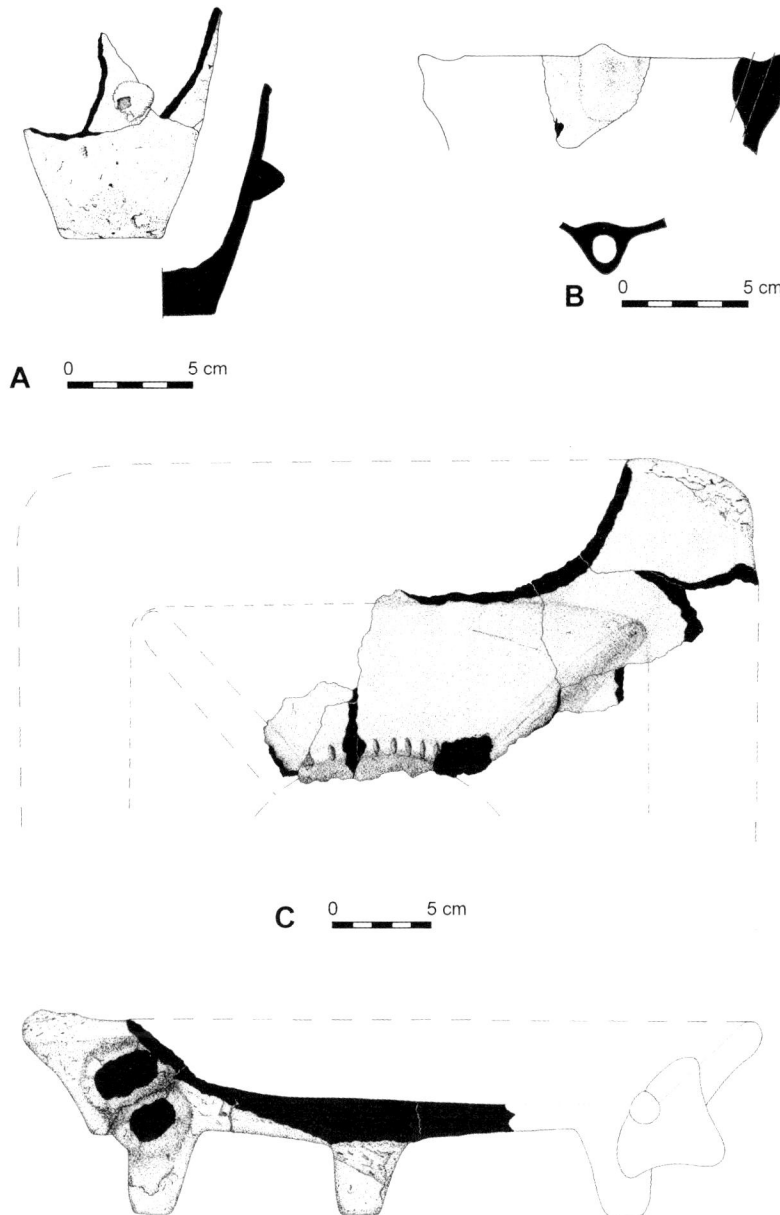

Fig. 7. Ceramic artifacts from Block 9, Feature 15 at Vésztő-Bikeri. A – flat vessel base with lug decoration, Unit 9-35; B – perforated "lug-spout" from rim of bowl or pot, Unit 9-68; C – "altar" fragment, Unit 9-76. Drawings by Dóri Kékegyi, Munkácsy Mihály Múzeum, Békéscsaba, Hungary

the eastern feature contained a few ceramic vessels and several bone/antler projectile points that seem to have been burnt *in situ* when the house was destroyed (Fig. 8). The distribution of these materials suggests that the large structure contained discrete activity areas. For example, the several dozen antler and bone arrowheads (and debitage associated with their manufacture) found in Feature 4/14 were collected from a 1.5 m area within the western half of the structure. A few

Fig. 8.   Antler points from Block 2 at Vésztő-Bikeri, Feature 4/14, Unit 2-94, SF 60. Top – obverse view; Bottom – converse view. See also Parkinson *et al.* (2004:111, figure 7) for drawings of more antler points. Photograph by Barrett Doran, Utah State University

meters east of the area where the arrowheads were discovered, a small collection of nearly identical mugs were found (Fig. 9). And a few meters east of that, several large storage vessels were recovered.

The structure in Block 3 (Feature 5) was oriented northwest–southeast and we have identified only one of its wall trenches. In contrast to the structure in Block 2, the structure in Block 3 contained a large deposit of ceramic vessels and several artifacts associated with textile manufacture (Figs. 10–11). A child burial was found just outside the Feature 5 wall trench.

Just to the south of the structures at the center of the site, we opened a 2-x-2 m unit to explore a magnetic anomaly Sarris had identified as a "thermal feature" (Sarris, 2003). Our excavations in Block 8 revealed a series of small rectangular kilns or ovens (cf. Killebrew, 1996) that were constructed in a deep (ca. 1.5 m) bell-shaped pit

that was filled with burned daub fragments. The pit may have been excavated and used as a well or cistern before it was filled with burned daub and eventually used as a kiln.

Preliminary analyses of flora and fauna collected from the settlement indicate a general continuation of the trends established during the Late Neolithic in the area. Preliminary analysis suggests that domestic species constitute over two-thirds of the identified animal bones from the site. Domestic cattle are represented by the highest number of identified bone fragments (NISP), but the remains of pigs, sheep, and goats also are common. Wild species include several fish and bird species, as well as roe deer, red deer, wild pigs, and aurochs (Parkinson *et al.*, 2004; Nicodemus, 2003). The majority of the floral remains are domesticates (Kasper, 2003), including barley (*Hordeum vulgare*), einkorn (*Triticum monococcum*), emmer wheat (*Triticum dicoccum*), bread

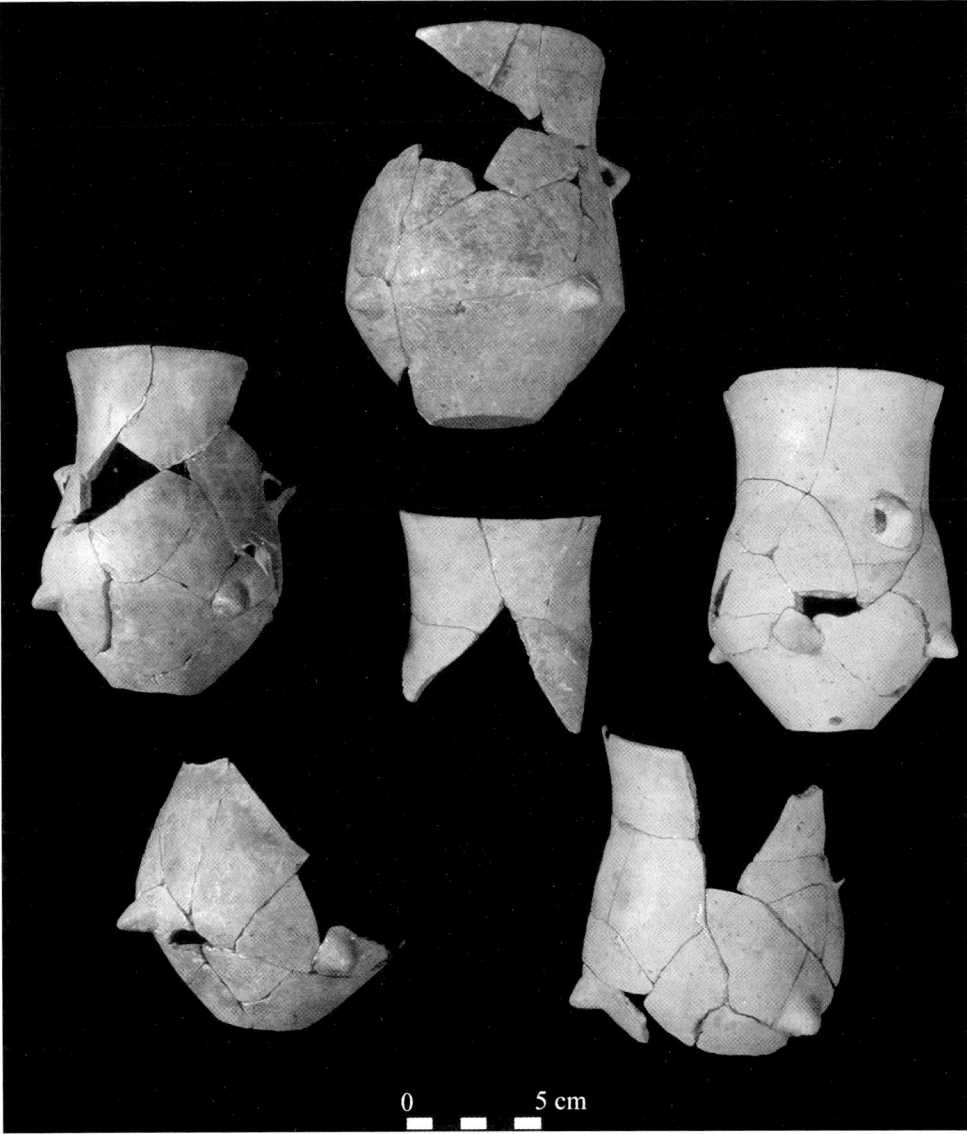

Fig. 9. Mugs from Block 2 at Vésztő-Bikeri, Feature 4/14, Unit 2-143. See also Parkinson *et al.* (2004:108, figure 5) for drawings of other artifacts from Block 2. Drawings by Dóri Kékegyi, Munkácsy Mihály Múzeum, Békéscsaba, Hungary

wheat (*Triticum aestivum*), and vetch (*Vicia* sp.). Wild plant species include cornelian cherry (*Cornus mas*), wild strawberry (*Fragaria vesca*), and plum or cherry (*Prunus* sp.).

We have argued that the organization of the settlement at Vésztő-Bikeri reflects a general trend towards intensification of production that occurs towards the end of the Neolithic in central and southeastern Europe (Kaiser and Voytek,

1983; Parkinson *et al.*, 2004; Tringham and Krstić, 1990). In particular, the distribution of discrete activity areas within the different structures in the settlement suggests that different households may have been carrying out different tasks. This differentiation at the household level suggests that the settlement as a whole became a functional, integrated, economic unit. This contrasts sharply with the organization of Late

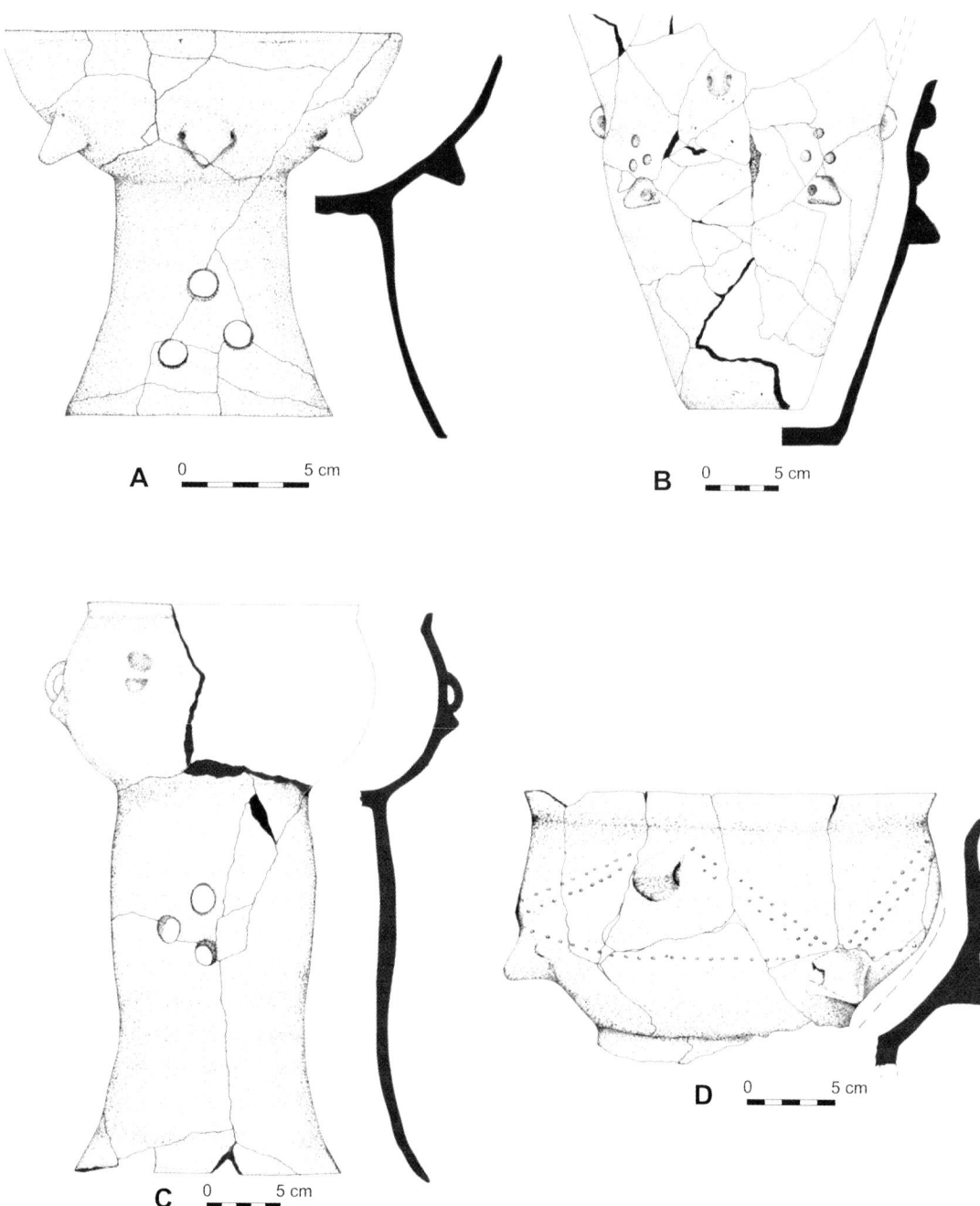

Fig. 10. Ceramic vessels from Block 3, Feature 5 at Vésztő-Bikeri. A – pedestalled bowl with lug decoration, pedestal is pierced, Unit 3-152; B – flat-based "flower pot" with restricted neck, lug and dotted-incised decoration, Unit 3-175; C – pedestalled bowl with slightly everted rim, pierced lug decoration, pedestal is pierced, Unit 3-189; D – pedestalled bowl with everted rim, dotted-linear incised and lug decoration, pedestal is missing, Unit 3-178. Drawings by Dóri Kékegyi, Munkácsy Mihály Múzeum, Békéscsaba, Hungary

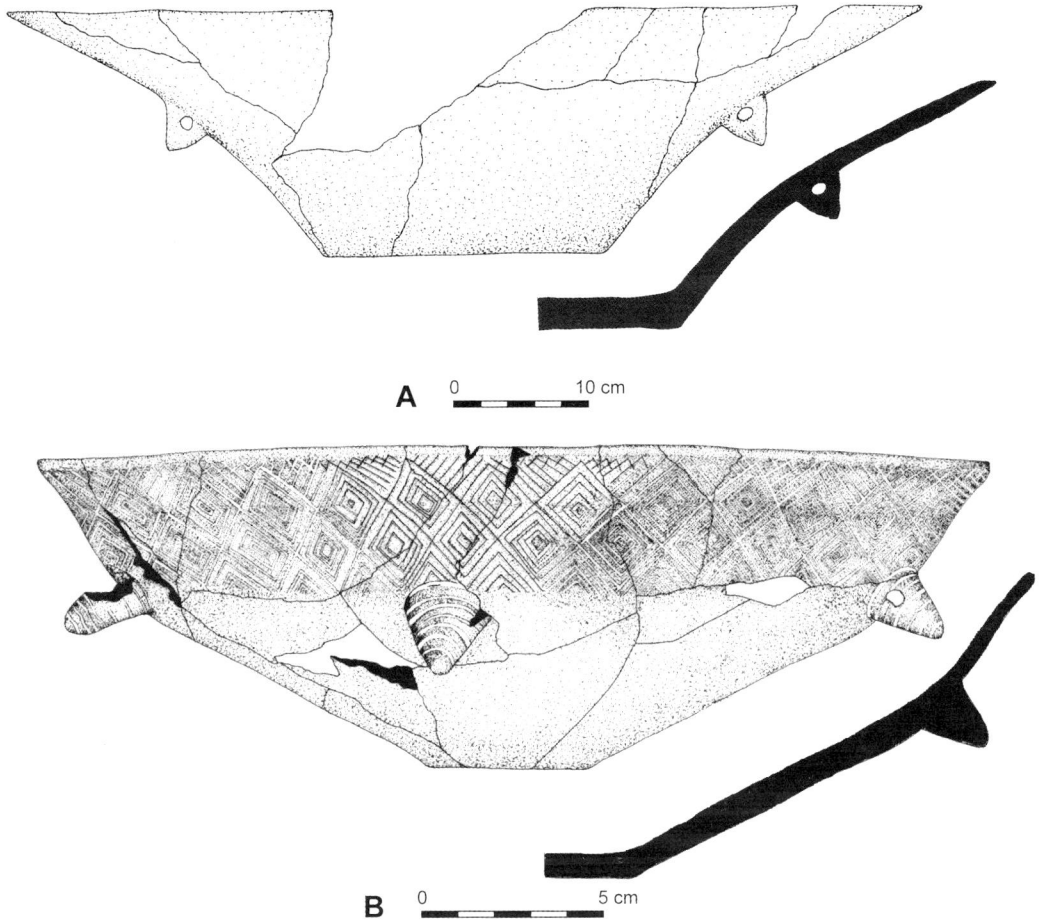

Fig. 11. Ceramic bowls from Block 3, Feature 5 at Vésztő-Bikeri. A – large flat-based bowl with straight flaring rim and lug decoration, Unit 3-173; B – flat-based bowl with meandric linear incision and white incrustation around rim, and pierced lug decoration with linear incision and white incrustation, Unit 3-64. Drawings by Dóri Kékegyi, Munkácsy Mihály Múzeum, Békéscsaba, Hungary

Neolithic settlements, which frequently were sub-divided into several discrete economic units (e.g., household clusters).

Investigations at Körösladány-Bikeri

The site of Körösladány-Bikeri (K-14) was identified by Hungarian researchers during the course of the Magyarország Régészeti Topográfiája surveys (Ecsedy *et al.*, 1982: 106) and was revisited in 1998 by the Körös Regional Archaeological Project (Parkinson, 1999: 201). Systematic surface collections revealed a more diffuse scatter of surface materials than at Vésztő-

Bikeri distributed over a slightly larger area. While the ceramic assemblage at Vésztő-Bikeri indicated it was a single-component Early Copper Age Tiszapolgár settlement, the material from Körösladány-Bikeri yielded a few ceramics that date to the Sarmatian (Iron Age) and Árpádian periods (end of the 1st millennium AD).

In 2001 we opened two 2-x-2 m test units at the northwestern edge of Körösladány-Bikeri where daub and Tiszapolgár ceramics occurred in highest frequency on the surface (Fig. 3). Unlike our test excavations at Vésztő-Bikeri, which came down directly on intact structural remains, the test units at Körösladány-Bikeri revealed only a

cultural layer beneath the plowzone with no iden-
tifiable features.

In 2003 Apostolos Sarris conducted a magnetometric survey at Körösladány-Bikeri that yielded a settlement organization similar to that at
Vésztő-Bikeri, with circular anomalies that enclosed an area ca. 0.7 ha (Fig. 3; Sarris, 2004).
Within these circular anomalies the remote sensing also identified several rectilinear and circular
anomalies concentrated at the center of the site.
These patterns were bolstered by analyses of soil
phosphate levels which were higher near the circular anomalies and lower towards the center of
the site, where the rectilinear features are concentrated (Fig. 4; Hardy, 2004; Lee *et al.*, 2004).

Based on our confirmation of similar geophysical patterns through excavation at Vésztő-
Bikeri, we are confident the circular anomalies
around the settlement at Körösladány-Bikeri are
associated with ditches and wall trenches that enclosed the settlement and that the rectilinear
anomalies at the center of the site are associated
with wall trenches from structures. Sarris (2004)
contends that the strength of the circular magnetic
anomalies at Körösladány-Bikeri indicates that
the stockade and ditches are deeper and wider
than those at Vésztő-Bikeri. In addition, the rectilinear anomalies within the settlement are significantly smaller than the structures identified by
magnetometry and confirmed by excavation at
Vésztő-Bikeri, suggesting that habitation at
Körösladány occurred in structures significantly
smaller than the longhouses at Vésztő-Bikeri.

The higher levels of soil phosphate at
Vésztő-Bikeri were associated with excavated
midden deposits that contained many faunal remains and refuse (including dung?) and we sus-
pect the high phosphate signatures at Körösladány-Bikeri are associated with similar cultural
deposits.

Spatial and chronological relationships
between the sites

The two sites are located less than 70 m apart,
and appear to have been on the same bank of a
paleo-meander of an ancient arm of the Körös
River. The canal that runs between the two sites
may be a modern feature. The paleo-meander of
the Körös runs just to the south of the two sites

(Fig. 2), suggesting both sites would have been on
the right bank of the ancient bed of the channel. If
this channel was active during the Copper Age it
would have winded to the west towards the Triple
Körös.

Chronologically, both sites are associated
with the Early Copper Age Tiszapolgár Culture.
Of the more than 80,000 Tiszapolgár ceramic
fragments collected from Vésztő-Bikeri, only a
handful show stylistic similarities with Late Neolithic Tisza and Herpály Culture sites in the region. Radiocarbon dates on charcoal and organic
remains from several features at Vésztő-Bikeri
concentrate between 4,500–4,200 B.C., suggesting it is nearly contemporary with the terminal
Neolithic phase (Herpály and Proto-Tiszapolgár
layers, Levels 5 and 6) at Berettyóújfalu-Herpály
(Fig. 12; Parkinson *et al.*, 2004: Table 2).

The late Neolithic (Tisza Culture) layers at
the nearby tell site of Vésztő-Mágor produced a
series of dates ranging from 6250–5970 bp (uncalibrated; see Kalicz and Raczky, 1987: 28), suggesting it was abandoned sometime before 4700
BC (calibrated). The most mature forms of Tisza
ceramics and the transitional Proto-Tiszapolgár
phase are not represented at Mágor, and the single
Early Copper Age radiocarbon date from the site
yielded a date of 4,360–4,050 B.C. (2 σ; see Parkinson *et al.*, 2004: 106), suggesting it may have
been occupied later during the Tiszapolgár period.
The site continued to be occupied into the Middle
Copper Age (Bodrogkeresztúr Culture).

In contrast to Vésztő-Bikeri, which is a single
component Tiszapolgár site, the material from
Körösladány-Bikeri produced some ceramics dating to the Sarmatian Period (second to fourth century A.D.). Most of this later material was concentrated northwest of the densest concentration
of Tiszapolgár material.

Although the artifacts from both sites can be
typologically associated with the Early Copper
Age Tiszapolgár Culture, the relative chronological relationship within that period between the
two sites remains ambiguous. The ceramic assemblages from both sites are nearly identical, with
typical Tiszapolgár vessel types, dominated by
bowls with everted rims and straight-walled pots,
both with flat and pedestal bases (Bognár-
Kutzián, 1963, 1972; Parkinson, 1999). Unfortunately, at this time we are unable to determine

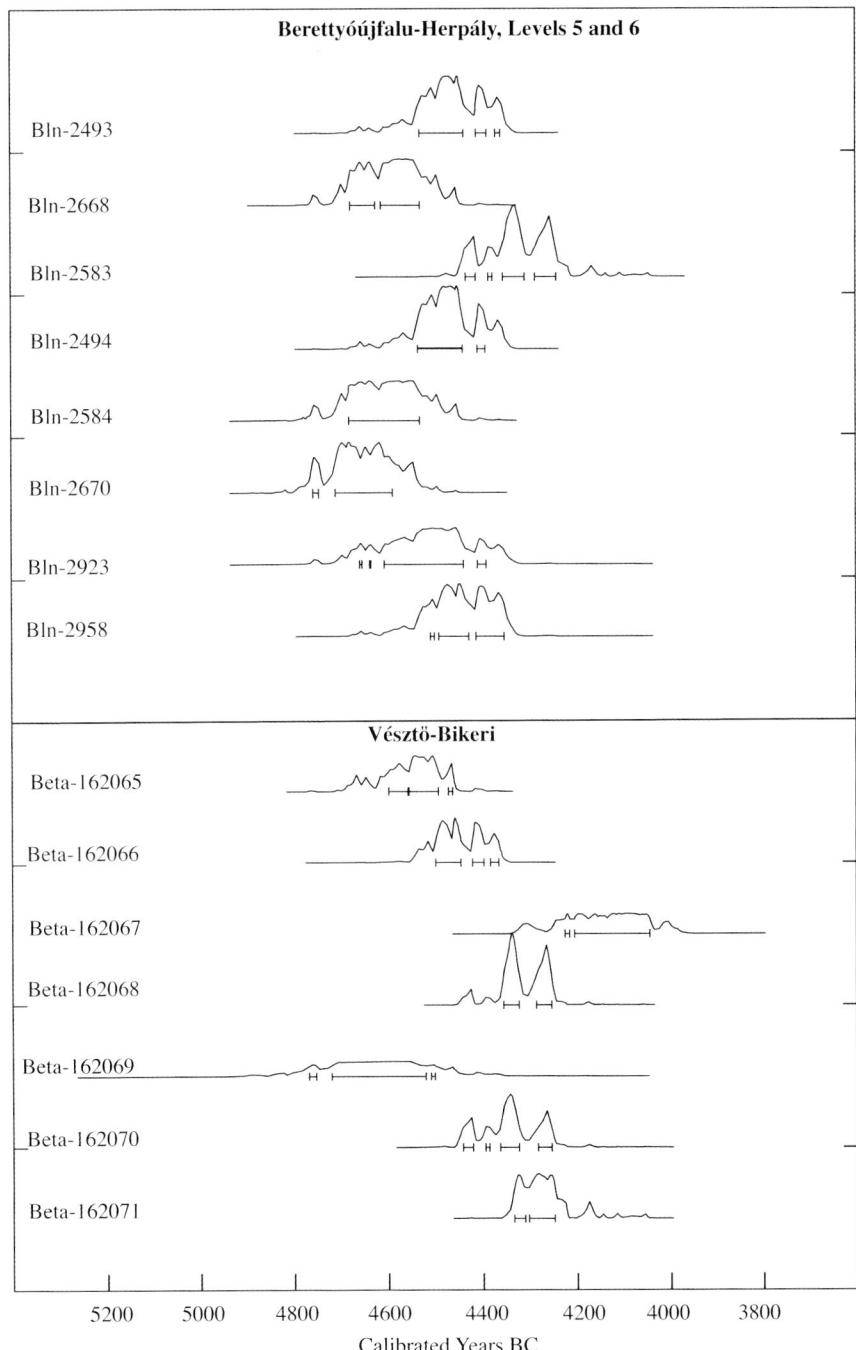

Fig. 12. Probability distributions (2 σ, 95.4% probability) for radiocarbon dates from Berettyóújfalu-Herpály (top) and Vésztő-Bikeri (bottom). Distributions from Berettyóújfalu-Herpály include samples from Levels 5 and 6, the Late Herpály and Proto-Tiszapolgár levels (Kalicz and Raczky 1987:29). The distributions from Vésztő-Bikeri are from various contexts across the settlement (Parkinson *et al.*, 2004:106). Probability distributions were generated using CALIB 4.4 (Stuiver *et al.*, 2004). For calibration information see Stuiver and Braziunas (1993), Stuiver *et al.* (1998a, 1998b)

based on the ceramic typology whether the sites were contemporaneous or whether one preceded the other within the Early Copper Age Tisza-polgár Period.

CONCLUSIONS

The results of our preliminary research offer an initial glimpse into the organization of Early Copper villages on the Great Hungarian Plain. Our results confirm some patterns that have been inferred or suspected for some time and have helped define other patterns that raise new questions and provide exciting avenues for future research.

The size of the Early Copper Age sites in the Vésztő cluster is small compared to most of their Late Neolithic counterparts in the region, lending support to the idea that the larger, nucleated, communities of the Late Neolithic fragmented and dispersed into numerous smaller villages. In northern Békés County, for example, the Magyarország Régészeti Topografiája reported 43 sites with Late Neolithic materials as opposed to 247 in the Early Copper Age (Ecsedy *et al.*, 1982; Jankovich *et al.*, 1989; Parkinson, 2002). The relative chronology of the settlements within both periods needs to be established, nevertheless the spatial organization of sites suggests that settlements were more frequently relocated in the Early Copper Age (Parkinson, 1999: 315).

Our research at the Early Copper Age settlements near Vésztő suggests that although the settlements are considerably smaller than Late Neolithic settlements in the area, such as the Vésztő-Mágor tell, they retain several features normally associated with the Late Neolithic. A high degree of labor was invested in the construction of the enclosures around the settlements and the buildings at the center of the settlements. In addition, the spatial and chronological relationships between the fortifications and the buildings at Vésztő-Bikeri suggest they were built simultaneously. This picture contrasts sharply with earlier models that suggested Early Copper Age settlements were more ephemeral than Late Neolithic sites and that the times were more peaceful (Bognár-Kutzián, 1972; Parkinson *et al.*, 2004).

While Early Copper Age settlements in the Körös region may have been smaller and occu-pied for shorter periods of time than Late Neolithic villages, some, such as the site of Vésztő-Bikeri were constructed with substantial investments of labor and inhabited long enough to develop incipient tell-like characteristics (see also Crna Bara; Bognár-Kutzián, 1972: 167). The radiocarbon dates from Vésztő-Bikeri suggest the site may have been inhabited for several generations, and we have documented at least two – and perhaps as many as four – construction phases at the center of the site.

The types of plants and animals that were being exploited during the Early Copper Age did not differ substantially from those that had been exploited in the Late Neolithic on the Great Hungarian Plain, but the social units within settlements may have become more integrated during the Early Copper Age. Parkinson *et al.* (2004) have suggested that the spatial patterning of activity areas within different structures at Vésztő-Bikeri may be indicative of a trend toward economic intensification that occurs throughout central and southeastern Europe towards the end of the Neolithic (Kaiser and Voytek, 1983; Tringham and Krstić, 1990).

Fortifications were thought to have become "superfluous" in the Copper Age (Bognár-Kutzián, 1972), but the magnetometric results, combined with our excavations at Vésztő-Bikeri, have demonstrated that both sites were surrounded by substantial walls and ditches. Although it is possible these features were "symbolic" enclosures, they have more substantial predecessors at Late Neolithic tell sites in the region that almost certainly functioned as fortifications (Raczky *et al.*, 1994, 2002). Similar features also have been excavated at Middle Copper Age (Bodrogkeresztúr Culture) sites in the region, although it remains unclear whether the circular features at those sites were associated with settlements or occurred in isolation (Makkay, 2001). While the precise functions of the ditches and stockades remain ambiguous, their occurrence at Vésztő-Bikeri and Körösladány-Bikeri establishes their continuity from the Neolithic through the Copper Age in the region. Rescue excavations at Kisrétpart and Bélmegyer-Mondoki also uncovered sections of ditches that may have had similar functions at those sites (Goldman, 1977; Siklódi, 1982). Remote sensing at the site of Ujvár (Uivar) in south-western Romania also documented similar featu- res around a much larger Copper Age settlement (Florin Drasovean, personal communication, 2001).

While Vésztő-Bikeri and Körösladány-Bikeri exhibit striking similarities in size and spatial organization, the size of domestic structures at both sites differs considerably. Whereas our excavations at Vésztő-Bikeri have verified the existence of longhouses there, the rectilinear magnetometric features at Körösladány-Bikeri are considerably smaller, suggesting a different form of household organization at that site. The early absolute dates of the longhouse structures at Vésztő-Bikeri indicate very close, if not overlapping, chronological and social affinities with Late Neolithic cultures in the region. By contrast, the smaller structures at Körösladány-Bikeri are more reminiscent of later Copper Age and Bronze Age settlements. We propose that the settlement at Körösladány-Bikeri was occupied later in the Early Copper Age than the settlement at Vésztő-Bikeri. If our excavations in the next few years demonstrate this to be the case, then we will have good evidence that the dispersal of settlement at the end of the Neolithic preceded the reorganization of the household units, thus allowing us to parse apart the social processes that seemingly changed abruptly at the end of the Neolithic.

Acknowledgements

The research described in this article was supported with generous funding from the National Science Foundation Research Experience for Undergraduates- Sites Program (NSF 0243583), a National Science Foundation International Cooperative Research Grant (NSF 0105851), and a grant from the Hungarian National Academy of Sciences (OTKA). Ms. Morris participated on the REU field school as an undergraduate student, and we thank her and the dozens of other students who have participated on the project over the years. Dóri (Q-kac) Kékegyi prepared the drawings. Köszi, Dóri! Barrett Doran photographed the artifacts. We also wish to thank the other experts and specialists who have contributed to the project directly and indirectly, including Michael Galaty, Katalin Hegedűs, Ferenc Horváth, Dóri Kékegyi, János Makkay, Pál Raczky, and Imre Szatmári. Finally we want to thank our good friends in Vésztő, without whom our research would not be possible.

REFERENCES

BÁNFFY E. 1994. Transdanubia and Eastern Hungary in the Early Copper Age. *A Jósa András Múzeum Évkönyve* XXXVI, évfolyam edition, A Nyíregyházi Jósa András Múzeum, Nyíregyháza, Hungary, 291–296.

BÁNFFY E. 1995. South-West Transdanubia as a mediating area. On the cultural history of the Early and Middle Chalcolithic. In: B. M. Szőke (ed.) *Archaeology and Settlement History in the Hahót Basin, SW-Hungary, ANTAEUS: Communicationes ex Instituto Archaeologica Academiae Scientiarum Hungaricae 22.* Archaeological Institute of the Hungarian Academy of Sciences, Budapest, 157–196.

BOGNÁR-KUTZIÁN I. 1963. *The Copper Age cemetery of Tiszapolgár-Basatanya.* Archaeologica Hungarica. Akadémiai Kiadó, Budapest.

BOGNÁR-KUTZIÁN I. 1972. *The Early Copper Age Tiszapolgár Culture in the Carpathian Basin.* Archaeologica Hungarica. Akadémiai Kiadó, Budapest.

BÖKÖNYI S. 1988. *History of domestic mammals in central and eastern Europe.* Akadémiai Kiadó, Budapest.

CHAPMAN J. 1997. Changing gender relations in the later prehistory of eastern Hungary. In: J. Moore and E. Scott (eds.) *Invisible people and processes: Writing gender and childhood into European archaeology.* Leicester University Press, London, 131–149.

DEREVENSKI J.S. 1997. Age and gender at the site of Tiszapolgár-Basatanya, Hungary. *Antiquity* 71, 875–89.

ECSEDY I., KOVÁCS L., MARÁZ B., TORMA I. 1982. *Magyarország Régészeti Topográfiája VI. Békés Megye Régészeti Topográfiája: A Szeghalmi Járás (IV/1).* Akadémiai Kiadó, Budapest.

GIMBUTAS M.A.E., DEXTER M.R., JONES-BLEY K. (eds.) 1997. *The Kurgan culture and the Indo-Europeanization of Europe: Selected articles from 1952 to 1993. Journal of Indo-European studies. Monograph No. 18.* Institute for the Study of Man, Washington, DC.

GOLDMAN GY. 1977. A Tiszapolgári kultúra települése Bélmegyeren. *Archeologiai Értesitő* 104, 221–234.

GYUCHA, A., PARKINSON W.A., YERKES R. In press. Előzetes jelentés a Körös Regionális Régészeti Program 1998–2002 között végzett munkájárol. *Studia Archaeologica.* Revisions accepted, February 2004.

HARDY M. 2004. Report: Analysis of soil phosphates, Körösladány-Bikeri (K-14). Unpublished Manuscript, Department of Anthropology, Florida State University, Tallahassee, FL.

HEGEDŰS K. 1977. *A Vésztő-Mágordombi újkkori és rézkori temetkezések.* Ph.D. Dissertation, Institute of Archaeology, Budapest, Hungary.

HEGEDŰS K. 1982. Vésztő-Magori-domb. In: I. Ecsedy, L. Kovács, B. Maráz, and I Torma (eds.) *Magyarország Régészeti Topográfiája VI. Békés Megye Régészeti Topográfiája: A Szeghalmi Járás (IV/1)* Akadémiai Kiadó, Budapest, 184–185.

HEGEDŰS K. 1983. A Hegeds Katalin Vésztő-Mágoron végzett ásatásaiból származó leletanyag rendezése. Unpublished manuscript on file at Munkácsy Mihály Múzeum, Békéscsaba, Hungary.

HEGEDŰS K., MAKKAY J. 1987. Vésztő-Mágor: A settlement of the Tisza Culture. In: P. Raczky (ed.) *The Late Neolithic of the Tisza Region: A survey of recent excavations and their findings.* Szolnok County Museums, Budapest-Szolnok, 85–104.

JANKOVICH D., MAKKAY J., SZŐKE B. (eds.) 1989. *Magyarország Régészeti Topográfiája VIII. Békés Megye Régészeti Topográfiája: A Szarvasi Járás (IV/2).* Akadémiai Kiadó, Budapest.

JANKOVICH D., MEDGYESI E., NIKOLIN E., SZATMÁRI I., TORMA I. (eds.) 1998. *Magyarország Régészeti Topográfiája X. Békés és Békéscsaba (IV/3).* Akadémiai Kiado, Budapest.

KAISER T., VOYTEK B. 1983. Sedentism and economic change in the Balkan Neolithic. *Journal of Anthropological Archaeology* 2, 323–353.

KALICZ N., MAKKAY J. 1977. *Die Linienbandkeramik in der Grossen Ungarischen Tiefebene. Studia Archaeologica.* Akadémiai Kiadó, Budapest.

KALICZ N., RACZKY P. 1987. The Late Neolithic of the Tisza Region: A survey of recent archaeological research. In: P. Raczky (ed.) *The Late Neolithic of the Tisza Region.* Kossuth Press, Budapest-Szolnok, 11–30.

KASPER K. 2003. Macrobotanical analysis in southeast Hungary: The Vésztő-Bikeri Site. Unpublished Masters Thesis, Department of Anthropology, Florida State University, Tallahassee, Florida.

KILLEBREW A. 1996. Pottery kilns from Deir el-Balah and Tel Miqne-Ekron. In: J.D. Seger (ed.) *Retrieving the past: Essays on archaeological research and methodology in honor of Gus W. van Beek.* Cobb Institute of Archaeology, Mississippi State University, Starkville, Mississippi, 135–162.

LEE E., GALATY M., and HARDY M. 2004. Soil chemistry at the Körösladány-Bikeri Site. Paper presented at the 69th annual meeting of the Society for American Archaeology, Montreal, Canada.

MAKKAY J.A. 2001. *Die Grabenanlagen im indogermanischen Raum.* Makkay János, Budapest.

MAKKAY J.A. 2004. *Régészet a szűliföldön.* Makkay

János, Budapest.

MEISENHEIMER M. 1989. *Das Totenritual, geprägt durch Jenseitvorstellungen und Gesellschaftsrealität: Theori des Totenrituals eines kupferzeitlichen Friedhofs zu Tiszapolgár-Basatanya (Ungarn).* BAR International Series. No. 475. British Archaeological Reports, Oxford.

NICODEMUS A. 2003. Animal economy and social change during the Neolithic-Copper Age transition on the Great Hungarian Plain. Unpublished Masters Paper, Department of Anthropology, Florida State University, Tallahassee, FL.

PARKINSON W.A. 1999. The social organization of Early Copper Age tribes on the Great Hungarian Plain. Ph.D. dissertation, Museum of Anthropology, University of Michigan, Ann Arbor, Michigan.

PARKINSON W.A. 2002. Integration, interaction, and tribal "cycling": The transition to the Copper Age on the Great Hungarian Plain. In: W.A. Parkinson (ed.) *The Archaeology of Tribal Societies, Archaeological Series, No. 15.* International Monographs in Prehistory, Ann Arbor, Michigan, 391–438.

PARKINSON W.A., GYUCHA A., YERKES R. 2002. The Neolithic-Copper Age transition on the Great Hungarian Plain: Recent excavations at the Tiszapolgár Culture settlement of Vésztő-Bikeri. *Antiquity* 76, 619–620.

PARKINSON W.A., YERKES R.W., GYUCHA A. 2004. The transition to the Copper Age on the Great Hungarian Plain: The Körös Regional Archaeological Project excavations at Vésztő-Bikeri and Körösladány-Bikeri, Hungary, 2000–2002. *Journal of Field Archaeology*, 2002–2004, 101–121.

RACZKY P., MEIER-ARENDT W., KURUCZ K., HAJDÚ Z., SZIKORA Á. 1994. Polgár-Csszhalom: A Late Neolithic settlement in the Upper Tisza region and its cultural connections (Preliminary Report). *Jósa András Múzeum Évkönyve*, XXXVI, évfolyam edition, A Nyíregyházi Jósa András Múzeum, Nyíregyháza, Hungary, 231–240.

RACZKY P., MEIER-ARENDT W., ANDERS A., HAJDÚ Zs., NAGY E., KURUCZ K., DOMBORÓCZKI L., SEBŐK K., SÜMEGI P., MAGYARI E., SZÁNTÓ ZS., GULYÁS S., DOBÓ K., BÁCSKAY E., BIRÓ K., and SCHWARTZ C. 2002. Polgár-Csszhalom (1989–2000): Summary of the Hungarian-German Excavations on a Neolithic settlement in Eastern Hungary. In: R. Aslan, S. Blum, G. Kastl, F. Schweizer, and D. Thumm (eds.) *Mauerschau: Festschrift für Manfred Korfmann*, vol. 2. Greiner, Remshalden-Grunbach, 833–860.

SARRIS A. 2003. Technical Report: Geophysical Prospection Survey at Visztu, Hungary (2002). *Laboratory of Geophysical-Satellite Remote Sensing and Archaeo-Environment. Institute for Mediterranean*

Studies. Foundation of Research and Technology, Hellas (F.O.R.T.H.). Rethymno, Crete, Greece.

SARRIS A. 2004. Technical Report: Geophysical Prospection Survey at Körösladány 14–Visztu, Hungary (2003), *Laboratory of Geophysical-Satellite Remote Sensing and Archaeo-Environment. Institute for Mediterranean Studies. Foundation of Research and Technology, Hellas (F.O.R.T.H.).* Rethymno, Crete, Greece.

SARRIS A., GALATY M.L., YERKES R.W., PARKINSON W.A., GYUCHA A., BILLINGSLEY D.M., TATE R. 2004. Geophysical prospection and soil chemistry at the Early Copper Age settlement of Vésztő-Bikeri, southeastern Hungary. *Journal of Archaeological Science* 31, 927–939.

SHERRATT A. 1983. The development of Neolithic and Copper Age settlement in the Great Hungarian Plain, Part I: The regional setting. *Oxford Journal of Archaeology* 1, 287–316.

SHERRATT A. 1984. The development of Neolithic and Copper Age settlement in the Great Hungarian Plain, Part II: Site survey and settlement dynamics. *Oxford Journal of Archaeology* 2, 13–41.

SIKLÓDI CS. 1981. Szakdogozat: Eneolitikum a Közép-Tiszavidéken. Department of Archaeology, Eötvös Loránd University, Budapest.

SIKLÓDI CS. 1982. Előzetes jelentés a Tiszaug-Kisrétparti rézkori telep ásatásról. *Archeologiai Értesit* 109, 231–238.

SIKLÓDI CS. 1983. Kora rézkori település Tiszaföldváron. *Szolnok Megyei Múzeum Évkönyv* 1992–1983, 11–31.

SIKLÓDI CS. 1984. Bölcsészdoktori disszertacio: A Kisrétparti csoport. Department of Archaeology, Eötvös Loránd University, Budapest.

STUIVER M., BRAZIUNAS T.F. 1993. Modeling atmospheric 14C influences and 14C ages of marine samples back to 10,000 BC. *Radiocarbon* 35: 137–189.

STUIVER M., REIMER P.J., BARD E., BECK J.W., BURR G.S., HUGHEN K.A., KROMER B., MCCORMAC F.G., v.d.PLICHT J., SPURK M. 1998b. INTCAL98 Radiocarbon age calibration 24,000–0 cal BP. *Radiocarbon* 40:1041–1083.

STUIVER M., REIMER P.J., BRAZIUNAS T.F. 1998a. High-precision radiocarbon age calibration for terrestrial and marine samples. *Radiocarbon* 40: 1127–1151.

STUIVER M., REIMER P.J., REIMER R., 2004. CALIB 4.4 Online Edition. http://radiocarbon.pa.qub.ac.uk/calib/calib.html. Quaternary Isotope Lab, University of Washington, Seattle, WA.

TRINGHAM R., KRSTIĆ D.S. 1990. Conclusion: Selevac in the wider context of European prehistory. In: R. Tringham and D.S. Krstić (eds.) *Selevac: a neolithic village in Yugoslavia.* Cotsen Institute of Archaeology, University of California Los Angeles, Los Angeles, California, 567–616.

Guidelines for Authors

1. The aim of this journal is to publish lengthy site reports (including preliminary site reports) and other data-based articles (not syntheses), and to provide space for many illustrations.

2. Please include the radiocarbon information with your article. When citing dates, the date should be cited as BP calibrated or BP uncalibrated. You must cite the software used for calibration and the lab number. C14 dates and their locations should be marked where appropriate on the illustrations.

3. Please use metric units of measure.

4. For review and editorial purposes, please send 3 copies of the manuscript, 3 **photocopies** of the figures, and 3 **photocopies** of the tables, along with an electronic copy of the paper in Microsoft Word on a 3.5 inch floppy disk, CD, or 100 MB zip disk. Be sure to keep an electronic copy and a paper copy of your article and illustrations.

Please send your manuscript packet to the USA editorial office to the attention of the Production Editor, Wren Fournier, who will consult with the Scientific Co-Editors and arrange for its review. The address is Wren Fournier, Harvard University, Peabody Museum, Cambridge, MA 02138, USA. Note: the editorial staff of *Eurasian Prehistory* will assist in editing the English text if necessary. Please mark diskettes with your name, the disk format (IBM or MAC), and the name of the software programs that you used for both the manuscript and any figures. The preferred software for manuscripts is Microsoft Word.

To prevent valuable figures from being lost in the mail, **please do not send original figures, photos, or drawings**. The originals will be requested once the paper is accepted for publication.

5. Organization of the manuscript:

Title page
– Title of the paper (not to exceed 90 characters).
– Author names, affiliations, addresses, fax numbers, and e-mail address for all authors.
– Abstract (not longer than 300 words).
– Keywords (7 words or less).

Article
Manuscripts must be written in English and all of the text must be double-spaced on A4 or 8.5 inch x 11 inch paper. Text should be in Times New Roman font, and divided into sections and paragraphs. Headings must be ranked, and this should be marked in ink in the left margin using roman numerals (i.e., I, II, III).

Figures and Tables
Illustrations, line drawings, graphs, and photographs are all considered 'figures'. Figures should be the width of one column, or two columns, and may not exceed 205 mm in height. Each figure must be cited in the text, and must be in a separate file and numbered consecutively with Arabic numerals (i.e., figure 1, figure 2). Computer prepared line drawings should be supplied as vector graphics using standard system fonts (Arial or Times New Roman) and using line shading rather than tints. The preferred vector graphics software is CorelDraw 5-9. Computer prepared photographs should be submitted at publication size in TIFF format at 600 dpi. Do not use word processing programs to produce figures, drawings, or graphs, or to embed graphics into the text. If after your article is accepted you plan to submit original 'hard copies' of figures, please consult with the USA editorial office regarding specifications for submission and mailing. Please include a legend, a directional arrow, a title and a caption for each figure, and letter each item in the figure (i.e. a., b., c.).

Each table must be cited in the text, preferably in Arial font, and must be in a separate file and numbered consecutively with Arabic numerals (i.e., table 1, table 2). Tables usually just contain headings and numbers, however tables with graphic elements must be prepared with graphics software (for example, CorelDraw). Do not embed tables into the text. Please include a title and a caption for each table.

Acknowledgements
Please use the full name of universities or organizations and do not abbreviate.

References
The reference list should contain only the references that appear in the text. Please cross-check the text with the reference list to ensure the accuracy of spellings and dates, and ensure that all of the references that appear in the text appear in the reference list and vice verse. Papers that have not been accepted for publication may not be cited. Do not abbreviate the names of journals, books, publishers, or cities. When referring to tables and figures in cited papers, please use lower case (for example, Smith, 1961 fig. 3, tab. 6). References in

the text should be cited as: (Smith, 1988), using letters to indicate additional publications from the same year i.e. (Smith, 1998; Jones 1965a, b). For two authors, please name both i.e. (Smith and Jones, 1999). For three authors or more, please name the first author followed by *et al.* i.e. (Smith *et al.*, 2000). The reference list should appear in alphabetical order. You must spell out the full name of the article and the publication. Please follow the style of the journal ***Eurasian Prehistory***. Examples are below:

JONES M. R. 1965a. Bridles in Georgia. In: *Horsegear of the Eighteenth Century*. James Publishing, New York.

JONES M.R. 1965b. *Tapestries as horse blankets*. Johnson Publishing, Trenton.

SMITH A. V. 1998. Styles of horseshoes in Poland. *Antiquity* 22, 10-15.

SMITH A. V., JONES M. R. 1999. Boots with spurs. In: Z. Mason (ed.) *Equestrians of the Eighteenth Century*. Miller University Press, Dallas.

SMITH A. V., JONES M.R., SIMPSON C. T., AN-DREWS G. P. 2000. Food and lodging: barns and elevated mangers of the eighteenth century and their affect on equine morphology. In: *Humans Housing Large Animals*. Conference Proceedings from the 53rd Annual Meeting of Osteologists, Chief Press, London, 32-65.

Once your manuscript is accepted:

Notification: You will be notified by e-mail.

Figures: If you are submitting the hard copy of figures rather than an electronic copy the following guidelines should be followed: photographs should be provided as sharp, glossy, black and white prints 20% larger than the final size. Special consideration for color photographs may be granted by the Editors based on production costs and in consultation with the publisher. Black ink drawings on good quality tracing paper or white board should be used. All scales should be in metric units.

Permissions: Permission for the use of figures must adhere to USA legal regulations. If you are using a figure that has been published, you must provide a written, signed letter from that journal or press granting permission for the figure to be used. Credit must be granted to the original illustrator or photographer in the figure caption.

Final Proofreading: Authors will receive a typeset copy for final proofing. At that point, only corrections to the printer's errors will be accepted. Authors will receive 25 free reprints of their article. Further reprints may be published in batches of 100. Artwork will be sent to the first author one month after publication.